THE MYSTERY
OF MEN

By the same author

THE SECRET LEMONADE DRINKER
I HAVE A COMPLAINT TO MAKE
THE SINNER'S CONGREGATION
THE NUDISTS
IN THE MIDDAY SUN
THE TAX EXILE
A VILLAGE CALLED SIN
THE COMEDY HOTEL
THE HOLIDAY

THE MYSTERY OF MEN

GUY BELLAMY

LONDON NEW YORK SYDNEY TORONTO

This edition published 1996
by BCA
by arrangement with Simon & Schuster Ltd

Copyright © Guy Bellamy, 1996

CN 5800

Printed in England by Clays Ltd, St Ives plc

For KATE

Men are as chancy as children in their choice
of playthings.

Rudyard Kipling *Kim*

Men are unwise
and curiously planned.

James Elroy Flecker *Hassan*

The more I see of men, the more I admire dogs.

Mme de Sévigné

I

The man in the grey tracksuit and trainers who jogged along a sunlit lane inhaling air refreshed by maple and sycamore nurtured one grand illusion as he counted the painful miles of his daily run: before he was carried off, blind and mad, to a home for the terminally aggrieved, he would discover fragments of joy on this disordered planet and make the most of them.

It seemed a modest enough ambition, but events conspired to render these notional moments of pleasure strangely elusive, and the time that would otherwise be available for their enjoyment was filled by demands that were more urgent and less pleasant.

He ran on between green fields, watched by Friesian cows who gazed curiously at the expense of so much energy. He wondered about it himself sometimes, particularly during the third mile, but he had embraced this keep-fit mania two years ago on his fortieth birthday, believing it made him impervious to the little misfortunes that put other men on their backs, often for good. Three miles every evening and two visits a week to the gym were intended to intimidate the germs and viruses who would be persuaded to seek more vulnerable targets elsewhere. But it was not possible for him to overlook the fact that death struck the fit and the unfit impartially, or that if your vehicle left the road for whatever reason at eighty miles an hour the amount of time that you had previously devoted to jogging would not help when your car folded violently against a brick wall.

Black thoughts accompanied his exertions, bleak reflections on the disappointing past, the evaporating present and the unpromising future. He ran down a winding track of mud and gravel and out into the sunlight of a country lane. Between here and his home was the drinks station, a battered old hostelry called the Oasis of Sanity, and he pulled up, ran fingers through his blond hair and went in for his orange juice.

The tiny bar, all oak beams and brass ornaments, had only one customer this early in the evening. He sat at the counter with a half-empty pint mug in his hand and a Qantas airline sticker on his white short-sleeve shirt that said '*Please wake me for meals.*'

'Julian the jogger,' he murmured, belying the sticker's implication, 'still deluding himself that he'll live longer by wearing himself out.'

The man in the grey tracksuit, who was called Julian Wyatt, sat on a stool and fingered his pulse. 'Drink?' he asked.

'It'd be rude not to,' said the other man, emptying

his glass. 'I gave up drinking once. What a long day that was.' He took the newly-filled glass from the ravishing brunette who dispensed alcohol here and looked with distaste at Julian Wyatt's orange juice. 'The beneficial effect of exercise versus the beneficial effect of alcohol,' he said. 'Should we have a little bet on who'll live longer?'

Julian Wyatt, feeling no beneficial effect at all from his three-mile run which seemed to have drained his mind as well as his body, stared vacantly at the other man who lolled comfortably on his stool. He was overweight and bald, but two years younger than Julian Wyatt who was peevishly aware that Oscar Mansfield, with gleaming eyes and rosily-coloured cheeks looked in better health than himself.

'And how,' he asked eventually, 'would you collect a gambling debt from a corpse?'

'Therein lies the problem,' said Oscar Mansfield, smiling at the challenge. 'I'll work on it.' He lit a long cigarette with a yellow disposable lighter and reached for an ashtray on the counter. 'My father gave up cigarettes at eighty after reading that they shorten your life. It was a mistake. Deprived of the consolation of nicotine, he died at eighty-two. It took me three years to drink his Scotch.'

'You come from a family that keeps a keen eye on its health, I see,' said Julian Wyatt.

'And lives to be eighty-two. I'm genetically disposed to longevity. Your bet would have no chance despite this incessant running.'

3

Julian Wyatt drank his orange juice and contemplated an inexorable slide towards financial embarrassment. Running seemed to weaken his resilience, and orange-juice drinkers missed the optimism induced by alcohol.

'The prospect of death is the least of my worries, Oscar,' he muttered. 'I hardly ever think about it.'

'Ah, now we're getting somewhere,' Oscar Mansfield said. 'What is the *numero uno* anxiety that brings those furrows to your brow? The lovely Lavinia and her generous ways?'

'In what way generous?' Julian Wyatt inquired suspiciously.

'Not in the way you imagine,' said Oscar Mansfield sadly, 'although my availability has never been in question. I was referring to her capacity to spend money. Drunken sailors seem niggardly alongside her, I'm told.'

'She *does* seem to spend rather more than she needs,' Julian Wyatt conceded. 'A lot of it goes from the supermarket to the bin without ever seeing the microwave. It's just the buying that she enjoys.'

Oscar Mansfield shook his head at such mindless extravagance. He had to see a much-needed addition to his life when he parted with money, and was alarmed at the idea that some people would find spending an end in itself.

'In that case,' he said, 'I trust your business thrives and your investments boom. How are your shares doing?'

The painful expression which surfaced on Julian Wyatt's face suggested that this optimistic declaration strayed some way from the truth. 'My business doesn't thrive,' he said in measured tones, 'I have no investments and as for shares, please don't mention them. They have an unhappy history in my family. They practically destroyed my father.'

Oscar Mansfield perked up at this piece of news. 'Destroyed him?' he echoed. 'How could they do that?'

Julian Wyatt sipped his orange juice. 'Didn't I ever tell you? He bought £400-worth of shares once at an old fourpence ha'penny. They went up to one and sixpence and he made about a thousand pounds profit when a thousand was a lot of money.'

'This sounds like a happy story,' said Oscar Mansfield.

'We're only halfway through it. After he had sold them they went up to £100 each. Do you remember Poseidon? If he'd hung on to them a bit longer he would have made over two million pounds. It finished him. He used to burst into tears for no apparent reason and couldn't talk about anything else. It was like some men are ruined by a woman. That's the Wyatt family's experience of the stock market. Kindly don't raise the subject again.'

Oscar Mansfield shook his head once more in numb wonderment at such misfortune. 'My father went into the Futures market and did his boots on pork bellies,' he said. 'But we're not bound by the failures of our fathers, are we? That's what evolution's all about.'

'Pork bellies?'

'Bacon to you. He was gambling in the commodities market on the future price of bacon.'

'Your family seem to have a bizarre taste in bets as well as being negligent about its health,' said Julian Wyatt, happy to drop the subject. He had almost finished his drink and was ready for the tuna salad that was waiting for him at home if Lavinia had exhausted her craving for shops and still had the strength for routine domestic duties. She would tell him what she had spent in some glittering salon and he would tell her what he had borrowed in the gloomy entrails of a bank and they would marvel at the disparity of it all and then blank out the future with a stirring video.

He put down his empty glass and made to move, but Oscar Mansfield was frowning at his beer, deep in thought, in a manner which suggested that a statement loomed.

'I've got it,' he said. 'I've worked it out — how you collect a gambling debt from a corpse.'

'Terrific,' said Julian Wyatt, standing up. 'I'm going. My salad'll be getting cold.'

'Sit down,' said Oscar Mansfield. 'Let me run this past you. We each insure our lives and the survivor gets the money.' He smiled triumphantly. 'The corpse pays!'

'It would amount to insuring someone else's life, and I don't think you can do that,' Julian Wyatt said, sitting down again. 'It's an incentive to homicide.'

The frown returned briefly and then faded. 'We form

6

a Trust! Put the policies into a Trust and we are the two trustees. It's easy. Shall I make some inquiries?'

'By all means,' said Julian Wyatt. 'You don't look that fit to me. Do you fancy a jog tomorrow?'

'I'd sooner swim in a sewer, thanks. Kind of you to ask though.'

When Julian Wyatt had gone Oscar Mansfield marvelled at how old he looked. The man was forty-two but he had the face of a fifty-year-old. All that running was wearing him out. It was the same with sportsmen. The twenty-year-olds looked as if they were thirty and the thirty-year-olds looked as if they were ready for less strenuous pursuits. If Julian continued to run and to age at his present rate, a joint life-insurance scheme would be a cast-iron investment, yielding early dividends.

Sitting alone with his half-empty glass, Oscar Mansfield explored his idea, its complications and ramifications, and almost immediately a more ambitious plan bubbled to the surface of his inventive mind. Why should there only be two people in this syndicate? Why not three? Four? Five? The chances of an early death and an early pay-out increased proportionately with each new member. Of course, the money would be shared but shared money was better than no money. He considered candidates, hoping specifically to call up a few middle-aged men with a medical history that would provide hope for him without unduly alarming an insurance company, bored men with a tenuous grip on life who could afford the premiums. He was writing some likely names on the back of an envelope when Jones came in.

'Hallo Vernon,' he said, stuffing the envelope into his pocket. 'How fairly pleasant to see you.'

Jones, a tall man with a black moustache and mournful eyes, acknowledged the ambiguity of this greeting with the merest twitch of his mouth. He looked at the world with sorrow and anxiety, finding nothing to justify the hopes that nourished and sustained other people. For some years now it was only an obsessive interest in suicide that had kept him going.

He ignored the stools and leant with both hands on the bar, studying the drinks which might improve his mood. He wore brown corduroy trousers and a loose blue sweater, the uniform of a lecturer which in fact he was. Oscar Mansfield watched him, assessing the advantages, if any, of buying Jones a drink. The jokes came thin and slow when Jones was in the bar, but tonight the lugubrious beanpole had two words written all over him: syndicate member!

'What will you drink?' he asked. 'How are you, anyway?'

'I've been a lot more relaxed since I gave up hope,' said Jones. 'I'll have a whisky.'

'That should help in both departments,' said Oscar Mansfield, producing his wallet. 'I become very relaxed and hopeful after whisky.'

The ravishing brunette, who was called Fay and who had been busying herself restocking shelves behind the counter, rose to her feet to take the order. She and her husband had only recently bought this establishment and spending her working hours among men who happily confused their brains with alcohol was still a novelty.

'You missed your vocation, Vernon,' said Oscar Mansfield, offering the newcomer his whisky. 'With your demeanour you should have been a monk.'

'A monk?' said Jones, sipping his drink. 'Vows of poverty, celibacy and obedience. It sounds just like marriage to me.' He pulled a packet of cigarettes from his pocket but did not offer one. 'Have you ever thought of suicide?' he asked.

'Suicide?' said Oscar Mansfield, startled. The idea that Jones might top himself was a matter of supreme indifference to him, but he seemed to remember reading somewhere that it could invalidate an insurance policy. 'You don't think about things like that, do you? Suicide's bloody dangerous.'

'It's catching on,' said Jones, 'and four out of five are men. A solicitor disembowelled himself with a bread-knife last week. People are increasingly seeing it as The Answer.'

'If that's the answer, what's the question?' asked Oscar Mansfield, but Jones was staring thoughtfully into his whisky. His fascination with suicide had grown apace since his fortieth birthday five years ago, when certain targets and hopes and ambitions had grown fainter, shifted by the encroaching years from the realistic to the improbable. It seemed to him to be the way to go, taking the delicate sub-ject of his departure out of the hands of others — drunken drivers, over-worked doctors, midnight intruders — and placing it firmly where it belonged, in his own.

No article on the subject had escaped his attention, and he had a scrapbook of cuttings on suicides that had made the newspapers. Books were harder to find and once when a pamphlet had been published advising people on the most congenial methods of departing this world, the government, evidently frightened of losing voters, had banned it. But now the Japanese had produced a book, *The Complete Manual of Suicide*, and more than half a million copies had been sold very quickly.

Suicide, it seemed to Jones, had a certain cachet in that aggressive archipelago. It brought approval, recognition and prestige. But although, paradoxically, it was in these respects a good career move, the gesture was fatally flawed in that it seriously hindered the possibility of promotion.

The book discussed eleven ways of killing yourself, including freezing, poisoning, electrocution, drowning, hanging, self-immolation and jumping from a great height. It was quite specific about jumping from a great height. To ensure death you needed a fall of at least twenty metres. One floor equalled about three metres so in a typical building you should jump from the seventh or eighth floor. It was important, too, to make sure that the ground was clear of shrubbery. There was no point in bouncing around in a bush.

Jones did not like heights. His recurring nightmare had him cornered on the roof of a skyscraper with firemen peeping over the edge and offering him ladders. A much better method of going, and evidently the author's favourite, was freezing to death, or hypothermia, which was almost painless. All you had to do was take off all your clothes, wet your body and go out one night and lie on the lawn. A few drinks first would accelerate the death process as alcohol expanded the blood vessels and reduced body temperature. This method was best attempted, said the book, when you were hungry and tired.

Vernon Jones wasn't sure how Gaynor would react if she discovered a naked corpse on the lawn in the morning covered with frost, particularly if he had his customary early morning hard-on, and he didn't think, when the time came, that this would be the route that he chose. He had never liked the cold and waited hopefully for May every year. That was the problem with suicide – you had to endure a certain amount of unpleasantness first. Jumping in front of a train was a terrible mess, particularly if your clothes became entangled with the train and you were dragged along for a while. Hanging was listed as one of the more pleasant ways of dying, but it demanded a technical expertise involving body-weights and drops that he suspected he didn't possess.

He turned his mind from all this and considered Oscar Mansfield's inquiry.

'Is this as good as life gets? That's the question,' he said sombrely, puffing on his cigarette.

Oscar Mansfield stirred uneasily, wondering whether

he was about to be the only witness to a spectacular act of hara-kiri. Perhaps Jones carried upon his person a gun, a knife or a phial of pills, permanently equipped for a quick departure if the mood took him. He certainly talked that way.

'There's an old Latvian proverb,' he said, placing a restraining hand on Jones's arm.

'I bet there is,' said Jones, laughing mirthlessly. 'There's always an old Latvian proverb. What's this one?'

'A diamond is a piece of coal that stuck to the job.'

'What's that supposed to mean?' Jones looked at him suspiciously.

'Buggered if I know,' said Oscar Mansfield. 'Am I Latvian? I suppose it's pointing up the virtues of sticking at something. Persistence will be rewarded.'

'I'm forty-five, for God's sake,' said Jones irritably. 'How long have I got to persist?'

'As long as it takes,' Oscar Mansfield shrugged.

'As long as *what* takes?'

'Well, I don't know. What are you trying to do?'

'I'm trying to bloody enjoy myself,' said Jones with subdued exasperation. 'I'm trying to kid myself that this bloody nightmare is fun.'

'My God, Vernon,' said Oscar Mansfield, 'you certainly know how to brighten a man's evening. I can remember when people used to laugh.'

'I can remember when *I* used to laugh,' said Jones. 'I can remember laughing when they told me that schooldays were the happiest days of your life. Now

I'm beginning to think that they were right. What sort of world is it where the happiness is over by the time you're sixteen?'

'Is this why you returned to the schoolroom?'

'As it happens it was the job I was best equipped for,' said Jones, picking up his whisky.

Oscar Mansfield did not envy him his dreary existence in the academic corridors of higher education, lecturing, instructing, cajoling and correcting, nor did he think it was helpful to a man's personality. Jones could talk five languages and hadn't got anything interesting to say in any of them. Pedantry and power seemed to have erased every spark of hope, every scintilla of charm, and it was all too reminiscent of Oscar Mansfield's own interminable spell in a boarding school in the country where grey men droned irrelevantly, not caring whether or not they were heard. So far from feeling grateful to his old school, Oscar Mansfield bore an animosity and resentment that not even time could assuage.

'Why don't you get a decent job, Vernon?' he asked amiably. 'Teaching's not worth a pitcher of spit these days, is it? Like building igloos in the Sahara, and the kids all think that they've cottoned on to something that older people missed.'

'It's this secret knowledge that gives them the confidence to grow,' said Jones solemnly.

'And by the time they've discovered they're wrong, they've got kids of their own taking the piss out of them. That's the bit I like.'

He was surprised to hear Jones say anything in favour of today's fractious youths: he was like a burst balloon — you never knew which way he was going. It was time to pin him down.

'Listen, Vernon,' he said. 'I've had an idea and it could mean some tax-free money for you.'

Jones sat down. 'You have my attention but make it quick. It's just possible my wife is cooking me dinner.'

'We're going to form a syndicate, insure our lives and the money goes to the survivors.'

'And you think I'd be a pretty valuable member in a syndicate like that, do you?'

'Not if you're going to do yourself in. Insurance people don't like that sort of behaviour.'

'I could always disguise it,' said Jones. 'If I drive out of a side road into a lorry that's careering down the hill at sixty, I'm not a suicide, I'm a road fatality.'

'That would be very considerate,' said Oscar Mansfield. There was a sardonic side to Jones that he found difficult to handle.

'They only bring in a suicide verdict if they're quite certain. Otherwise it's an open verdict. Who's in the syndicate?'

'Julian Wyatt and me so far. We need four, I think.'

'I might be interested,' said Jones. 'You don't look too healthy to me. What will it cost?'

'I'm going to find out.'

'Right,' said Jones, standing up. 'Let me know.'

'I'll get back to you with the full scenario.'

Jones paused as he moved towards the door. 'That must be the worst sentence since "He makes me down to lie". In my class it would earn you extra work.'

When he had gone, Oscar Mansfied turned his attention to Fay who was now stocking a small fridge with bottles of fruit juice.

'Where's Colin?' he asked.

'Watching television. There's cricket on.'

'That's good. Could I borrow your body for half an hour? I'll look after it.'

Fay Dunbar, aged thirty, was now used to this sort of thing as to every other sort of thing that can happen to a pretty woman who tries to run a bar. It wasn't a job she had ever expected to do and two years earlier, when her husband was employed in the Byzantine world of computers, she managed a secretarial agency where the social life was much more civilised. Colin became a casualty of the recession at the very moment when the demand for secretaries began to dwindle, and the two of them thought for a month before deciding to put their capital into a rustic hostelry called the Oak Tree. To quash the idea that this was just another public house, they changed the name to the Oasis of Sanity, converted half the bar into a restaurant and hoped to spend most of their time catering for diners rather than drinkers. But it was a strange consequence of the continuing recession that people had given up eating but not drinking. And the most regular drinker was Oscar Mansfield who now said: 'Marry me, baby.'

'Oscar,' said Fay Dunbar with an obliging smile.

'We're both married.' She had black curls that fell over her face when she laughed, and a sunny nature that was an unquantifiable asset to the Dunbars' business venture.

'Couple of things you ought to know,' he murmured ingratiatingly. 'I've got thirty million in the bank and six months to live.'

'The longer I know you the more attractive you become,' Fay Dunbar said. 'Is there any documentary evidence to confirm this imminent clog-popping? It could be a bit of an anti-climax if you stuck around.'

At that moment Colin Dunbar emerged from the residential accommodation that lay at the back of the bar. He was a tall, good-looking man of thirty-five with dark wavy hair and an athlete's body.

'I could eat a horse if you spread butter on it,' he said. 'Good evening, Oscar. Are you our only customer?'

'There have been others,' his wife told him. 'We're still in business.'

'I don't think a flotation on the Stock Exchange is one of our immediate problems.' He sat on a stool behind the counter and pulled himself a half pint of lager. His bright yellow shirt had a Valentino label protruding from the side of his top pocket.

'It's more interesting than computers, though,' Oscar Mansfield suggested. 'The banter, the gossip, the rep-artee. What do you get out of your average computer buff? A glazed look and a mouthful of jargon.'

'Okay,' said Colin Dunbar. 'Hit me with some gossip. Lavinia's cat get run over?'

'This isn't gossip, more news,' said Oscar Mansfield. 'I'm going to form a syndicate with some of your customers in which we all insure our lives and the survivors share the loot. What do you think of that?'

Colin Dunbar looked puzzled. 'You selling insurance, Oscar? I thought you'd made your pile and quit.'

'Not selling it, organising it. Care to join in? A young healthy chap like you should clean up.'

'Who are the others?'

Oscar Mansfield told him and Colin Dunbar's face split into a huge grin.

'I should like to be part of this enterprise, Oscar. That jogging's putting years on Julian, Jones keeps talking about suicide and you look in need of a health farm.'

'You're in then?' said Oscar Mansfield, pulling out his envelope of names 'We seem to have a syndicate of four. Tomorrow I shall talk to some insurance people and see if we can set this thing up.'

'And what happens then?'

'We sit around and wait.'

2

A mansion in a park in the country had been leased by a leading assurance marketing group who, conducting their business by phone, post and fax, had found that the high rents and harrowing inconvenience of city life was harmful to their equanimity and quite unnecessary for their continued prosperity. Into their immaculate tarmac car park, surrounded by daffodils and lobelia, Oscar Mansfield drove his slightly worn BMW the following morning, and took his briefcase from the passenger seat before marching into the huge red-brick building in search of Mr La Fontayne.

What had once been a rich man's home had been transformed with no visible structural alterations into the insurance company's headquarters. Oscar Mansfield was escorted up a wide curving staircase that faced the main door and along a carpeted corridor by a young fresh-faced girl who had been sitting alone at a desk in the hall. She stopped at a door that bore Mr La Fontayne's name in gold italic letters and knocked twice.

Despite his exotic name, Mr La Fontayne looked as worried and oppressed as everybody else. He rose from a desk by the window, a small, balding man in an immaculate blue suit, and offered his hand.

'Mr Mansfield?' he said. 'This is an unusual idea. Take a seat.'

'Is it feasible?' asked Oscar Mansfield, lowering himself into a deep leather armchair. 'Is it legal?'

'It's feasible *and* legal,' said Mr La Fontayne, 'but is it ethical? You see, we'd have to be satisfied that the families were adequately catered for. In a sense that's what insurance is all about. We're a very *moral* business.'

'There are other policies that take care of the families. This is a private arrangement between four men. How could we do it?'

Mr La Fontayne consulted some notes.

'The easiest way to do it would be as you suggested, to put the policies in a Trust, with the other three as the trustees. It would have to be an Absolute Trust that can't be changed by any of you, and the nominated beneficiaries would be the trustees.'

Oscar Mansfield opened his briefcase. 'Let's talk about the premiums and the conditions,' he said.

Mr La Fontayne got up from his desk and went across to a computer on a table in the middle of the room. 'You want £100,000 on each death?' he asked.

'That's the idea.'

'If any of them are single, divorced or separated we'd want an HIV test.'

'None is.'

'Hazardous sports,' said Mr La Fontayne. 'Any deep-sea divers or addicts of hang-gliding?'

'None.'

'Okay, give me the details, one by one.'

'Well, there's me. Forty years old, married, no children of my own although my wife has one.'

'Smoker?'

'Yes.'

Mr La Fontayne punched keys on his computer and looked closely at the screen. '£105 a month,' he said.

'Jones,' said Oscar Mansfield, looking at the notes he had brought with him. 'Forty-five years old, smoker, no children but married.'

'£154.20 a month,' said Mr La Fontayne after a few moments.

'Julian Wyatt is forty-two, married, son of twelve, non-smoker,' said Oscar Mansfield. 'He's a keep-fit fanatic, weights and jogging.'

'£84.90,' said Mr La Fontayne.

'Finally there's Colin Dunbar who is thirty-five. Married, daughter of eight, non-smoker.'

'Fifty-one pounds and fifty pence. You spot the first problem here? The man who is most likely to collect the most pays the least, and the man — Jones, is it? — who is the least likely to collect, pays the most.'

Oscar Mansfield looked at the figures. 'We'll probably average it out so we all pay £100 a month. That covers it. How can Colin only be £51 a month, anyway?

If he lives to be seventy-five he'd only have paid you £25,000.'

Mr La Fontayne abandoned his computer and went back to his desk. 'That's the wonder of insurance for you,' he said with a smile. 'Have you thought of a ten-year policy, which would be much cheaper? What you're talking about is a "whole of life" policy where we, the insurance company, know that we'll have to pay up some day. But with a ten-year policy we might not have to pay at all so the premiums are much lower.'

'And two would drop dead after ten years and two weeks when we'd paid all that money,' said Oscar Mansfield. 'No thanks. What about medicals?'

'A medical attendance report from a GP is all we'd need. An M.A.R. we call it.'

Oscar Mansfield looked at his notes again and saw something that had been worrying him. 'What about suicide — does that invalidate it?'

'Not always. Obviously if somebody kills themselves two or three weeks after taking out a policy we wouldn't pay. But if it's two or three years we'd pay up. Why? Have you got a potential suicide in this quartet?'

'Who knows?' said Oscar Mansfield. 'We all have our gloomy moments.'

'Well, perhaps you'll find,' said Mr La Fontayne, 'that having the protection of a great insurance company round you will cheer them all up. Are you going ahead with this project?'

Oscar Mansfield stuffed his notes back into his briefcase, along with new notes that he had made during the conversation.

'I'm sure we will,' he said. 'I'll take your figures back to the others and see what they say.'

'How come I pay three times as much as Colin?' said Jones, whose highly-developed sense of persecution was not helped by the numbers that Oscar Mansfield had produced.

'You're old and decrepit and you've got the life expectancy of a dragonfly,' said Julian Wyatt.

'You're ten years older than me and you smoke, kid,' said Colin Dunbar. 'It's a miracle they're prepared to insure you at all.'

'If I'm that bad a risk, *you* can pay the premiums,' said Jones. 'I obviously don't stand to gain anything at all.'

'Come, come,' said Oscar Mansfield, anxious to hold this disparate group together. 'We all run the same risk every day of getting killed on the road or stabbed in the street. We all use trains and planes which manage to kill some of their customers every year. We can all wake up tomorrow with something going seriously wrong inside us.'

They were sitting in deckchairs on Oscar's lawn which, as its deep emerald green suggested, had been submitted to the various lawn-enhancing treatments that are to be found in garden centres. It had the thick texture of a well-made carpet.

23

Three phone calls had summoned his three guests to this Sunday afternoon conference, and the host was now trying to jolly them along with some blackberry whisky into accepting his grand idea of team insurance. His intuition was that although nobody shared his high enthusiasm for the idea, they were drifting towards agreement out of boredom.

'We might as well do it,' said Julian Wyatt, who was the only visitor to ignore the blackberry whisky. 'What have we got to lose?'

'About a hundred and fifty quid a month in my case,' said Jones. 'There's something grossly inequitable there.'

'I have a proposal about that,' said Oscar Mansfield, 'which is that we should all pay the same. It works out at ninety-nine pounds a month each. I know that means Colin is paying twice what the company wants from him, but he's best placed to make money out of the whole thing.'

'Fine,' said Colin Dunbar. 'I can't wait to have a piece of the action. Keep jogging, Julian. Study that suicide manual, Jones.'

'What happens if somebody can't pay the monthly premium?' Jones asked.

'We come round and blow your windows out,' said Julian Wyatt.

'People hit financial problems. They lose their jobs.'

'Not in your line of business they don't,' said Oscar Mansfield. 'When did you last hear of an unemployed lecturer?'

People always managed to give Jones the impression that being a college lecturer, with its generous pay, long holidays and dubious end product, placed him somewhere in the scheme of things between estate agents and child molesters, but he continued to hope that his lonely efforts would eventually be rewarded with some sort of acclaim, if not promotion.

'If anybody can't pay the premiums we obviously confer,' said Colin Dunbar. 'We help each other out to keep the thing going.'

'Exactly,' said Oscar Mansfield. 'It's a co-operative venture. We all stand together.'

'Until one of us falls over,' said Julian Wyatt. 'We withdraw our support if you expire. If you die, you're on your own. Death will be construed as resignation.'

'I think we get the picture,' said Jones, picking up his whisky. As the oldest man here, he felt less involved than the others, holding out no great hopes of picking up a tax-free £33,000 when the first shareholder perished. He had long passed that awful day when he realised that most people in the street were younger than he was, and his presence here this afternoon was not, like the others, motivated by the possibility of financial gain. The paucity of invitations in his humdrum life was more than enough reason to climb into his car when Oscar Mansfield offered him blackberry whisky on the lawn, and the syndicate itself held one irresistible attraction, humiliating though it was to admit it: he would have joined something and gained some friends. He refilled his glass and admired the aubrieta and alyssum in Oscar Mansfield's rockery.

Oscar himself sat back in his deckchair, the after-noon sun shining on his bald pate. He was wear-ing jeans and a somewhat grubby T-shirt which bore the slogan *I drink to make other people more interesting*. His white feet, splayed across his neat lawn, were only partly concealed by a pair of old sandals.

'How do we all feel about it?' he asked. 'Are we all in?'

His quest for a decision was temporarily thwarted by the urgent cry of a mobile phone that was ringing in Julian Wyatt's blazer pocket. He jumped out of his seat, dragged the phone from its hideaway and began to pace the lawn.

'Hi, David! How you doing?' he shouted. 'You get my figures?'

The others observed this technological miracle with palpable distaste, resenting both the intrusion and Julian Wyatt's possession of such an offensive trinket. It was some relief to them to see that it didn't seem to be making him happy.

'Jesus, David, don't do that!' he shouted into the phone, as if poor reception demanded a piercing tone. 'Look at the figures again. Look at the ones I've highlighted. We're talking crucifixion here.' His left hand covered his eyes while the right one held the phone to his ear.

'You carry a gadget like that around and you're

asking for trouble,' said Colin Dunbar. 'The trick is to keep the world away.'

Julian Wyatt's agitated tour of the lawn took him to the far end where a bank of roses and a wattle fence marked the boundary of Oscar Mansfield's acre, but his cries for help and his angry refutations of the conclusions of his caller drifted back to the others at sufficient volume to discourage conversation and even create some embarrassment. Eventually the phone was returned to his pocket, his shoulders slumped and he marched tensely back to his deckchair.

'Friend of yours?' asked Oscar Mansfield.

'My bank manager,' said Julian Wyatt. 'Or one of my bank managers.'

'Working on a Sunday?'

'A small commercial bank where the manager never stops working, not one of your big High Street variety. They're the people who lend the money these days. Or, in some cases, not.' He reached for his Evian water and emptied the glass as if it contained the consoling powers of alcohol.

Julian Wyatt had banks the way a dipsomaniac has bars, traipsing from one to another in search of satisfaction. Three years earlier he had been an account director in an advertising agency which successive government policies had brought to impressive profitability and then to the brink of collapse and finally to ruin. Julian Wyatt, who saved a bit in the good years, had retrieved from the wreckage at a knock-down price from the Receiver enough equipment — desks, chairs, Apple

Macs, colour photo-copiers, fax machines and queueing switchboards — to stock a small and busy office. From such cheap beginnings he felt that he had a head start if he could conjure up from the mists of the recession the business that would bring these assets to life, and so he formed Wyatt Promotions before going out to look for it. With the desks and the equipment he took a few people, too, who were grateful to move back so swiftly into gainful employment, but what he did not have from Day One were the hefty capital resources that his enterprise needed. A piece of business that would eventually net him £60,000 needed £40,000 immediately to finance it, and the £60,000 was always a long time coming. And so, while his busy staff sought customers, drew pictures, wrote blurbs, designed brochures, organised exhibitions, dreamed up advertisements and arranged favourable printing contracts all over the country, Julian Wyatt spent most of his time talking to cynical bank managers about the loans that he needed to keep his business alive. The words 'cash flow problem' were engraved on his heart, and the interest rates kept him awake. He could never understand why a business that was blessed with work and so intrinsically profitable was a continuing and horrifying financial nightmare.

He sat back in his deckchair and closed his eyes. The plan today was to get back from Oscar's early and give Lavinia one in the gazebo, but the phone call had blunted the ardour which he usually brought to his Sunday afternoon love sessions in the garden and he wasn't sure he was up to it.

'So what have we agreed while I was on the phone?' he asked wearily.

'Your anguished yelps made debate difficult,' said Oscar Mansfield. 'But now that peace has been restored, let's make a decision.'

'Let's do it,' said Colin Dunbar. 'I'll throw in a hundred a month.'

'Spoken like a thirty-five-year-old non-smoker,' said Jones. 'When was the last time you were ill?'

'Ill?' said Colin Dunbar, as if the word had no meaning for him. 'I had flu as a kid once. It went round the school.'

'Quite,' said Jones. 'I'm exposed to sneezing and coughing youths all day, not to mention, I imagine, dopeheads and intravenous drug-users. It's a wonder I haven't caught a galloping dose of something by now.'

'Get this policy into place quickly,' said Colin Dunbar. 'With an optimistic prognosis like that, we can't hang about.'

'Quite,' said Jones. 'You can all enjoy your world cruise while they cart me off to the crematorium.'

'Sounds fair,' said Julian Wyatt. 'Where do I sign?'

In Rose Cottage, the detached and extended home that stood at the end of the lawn, Emily Mansfield was writing a letter to the *Sunday Times*. She sat at a small table in the drawing room, with its bright light and beamed ceiling, and scribbled purposefully with her Parker pen on large sheets of blue paper. When her husband came in from the garden she looked up briefly.

'Friends gone?' He nodded and she asked: 'What were you talking about?'

'A little project.'

'That's good, dear,' said Emily Mansfield. 'You need something to do.'

Oscar Mansfield slipped out of the French windows to fetch the bottles and empty glasses from the lawn. He didn't think that he needed something to do at all; there were no gaps in his life that weren't already filled with pleasure. It was impossible for him to remember the last time he was bored.

He walked across the grass, looking for signs of encroaching moss, and then he bent down to see what damage had been done to it by the four deckchairs. The last time moss had appeared here he had killed it, scraped it up, sown grass seed and covered it with compost, and then waited an anxious month for the gaps on his lawn to be filled. He had always found something to occupy his time since a petrol company had arrived one memorable morning four years ago, brandishing a large cheque and suggesting with forceful charm that he sell the garage he had taken over from his father and run for most of his adult life. The garage had ticked over nicely with a staff of four but was never going to make him rich. The petrol firm, who wanted the site and not the garage, did that. Mansfield Mechanics, an esteemed local enterprise, vanished overnight and was replaced by a lurid green petrol station with neon lights, sweetshop and car wash, while Oscar went to London to discuss how best to invest his windfall, and then came home again in a daze to the delightful realisation that he had retired at thirty-six.

He moved the deckchairs back to the patio and then carried the glasses and bottles through to the kitchen. Rose Cottage was his pride and joy and he spent a lot of time looking after it. The thatched roof of combed wheat had recently been re-ridged, and his next project was to build a small barbecue at one end of the patio.

He returned to the drawing room where his wife was banging a stamp with perceptible satisfaction on to a large blue envelope. The name Emily Mansfield was not unknown to those curious souls who peruse the correspondence columns of newspapers. Her exasperated interjections, correcting the misguided proposals of politicians, questioning the vacillating beliefs of provocative churchmen, or merely denouncing the robustly articulated opinions of one of the newspaper's proliferating columnists, appeared regularly in a variety of publications. It was an activity that Oscar Mansfield found beyond his comprehension but it had this compensation: his wife felt a lot better when the letter had been written.

She stood up now with the deep satisfaction of a job well done. She was a small attractive woman of thirty-eight who seldom stopped moving. She seemed to be trying to compensate for the inactivity of her husband and had accordingly become involved in dozens of politically slanted activities. In his more pessimistic moments Oscar Mansfield thought that it was only a matter of time before she launched a Lesbian Mums'

31

Support Group. Once, after two or three brandies, she had alarmed him by describing children as a 'politically disadvantaged minority', and she showed a concern for distant races on the other side of the planet that, so far as Oscar could see, elicited neither profit nor gratitude.

But they had been married for only two years and he was still feeling his way into the difficult business of being a husband. Emily's first husband had turned into a woman, undergoing a sex-change operation in Casablanca, and Emily, who took it personally, had decided to find another. Marriage was not something that Oscar had ever found necessary to consider, but Emily had held a certain fascination for him ever since she regularly brought her old Golf to his garage. Her knowledge of cars extended up to but not beyond the fact that she had a clear idea what they looked like. The Golf she had owned for seven years before she worked out how to empty the ashtray. Sublime ignorance on this scale made for frequent visits to the garage and a relationship developed in more salubrious venues after work.

By the time that Emily's husband had been reassembled in North Africa and a second marriage had become a legal possibility, Oscar Mansfield, freshly enriched, prematurely retired and spending too much time alone in his splendid house, was finally amenable to the idea of a permanent companion.

He sat on the sofa wondering whether drinking

blackberry whisky was such a bright idea in the middle of the afternoon but then allowed himself the consoling thought that not all his ideas could be good ones.

3

At breakfast the following morning Emily Mansfield laid her *Daily Telegraph* alongside her scrambled eggs and said: 'You used to get eight years for rape, didn't you?'

'Who did?' asked Oscar, his mind on other things. He had told her at their very first breakfast together: 'Talk? I can't even spit in the morning.'

'Rapists,' said Emily, glancing sideways at her newspaper. 'Eight years. It was always eight years. Now they get three and sometimes it's a suspended sentence.'

'Well,' said Oscar, 'I don't really know what you expect me to do about that.'

'To get eight years now you have to rape two or three women. And you should do something about it. After all, it was you who voted for the so-called party of law and order.'

'I didn't vote for them for law and order, I voted for them because they were the only ones who wouldn't raise taxes.'

GUY BELLAMY

'Well, they have raised taxes, Oscar. Let that be a
lesson to you.'

'It is,' said Oscar, chastened. 'I'll never vote for the
bastards again.'

'Well, that's a start. Now, what are we going to
do about rapists?'

Oscar poured himself more tea. 'I'll leave that to you,
darling. I'm sure you've got plenty of notepaper left.'

'And what I'm going to say is that the sentences
should be laid down by Parliament, and not left to
the judges — most of whom have long since lost what
few marbles they started with.'

'That should do it,' said Oscar, sipping tea. 'Where
is our son and heir?'

'Adrian's still asleep. You get very tired at fourteen.
It's all that growing.'

Oscar Mansfield smiled — fondly, he hoped. He was
quite happy for Adrian to stay in bed and grow all
day. Being deprived of his interruptions, complaints
and demands was no hardship at all.

'And what about you?' asked his wife in her best
businesslike manner. 'What's your programme today?'

Oscar Mansfield finished his breakfast and looked
out of the window at a sky of unblemished blue. 'I'm
going to start work on the barbecue. You?'

'I'm going to an Oriental rug sale. A few little
purchases might brighten up the home.'

'My idea of brightening up the home is somewhat
cheaper, like putting pink toilet rolls in the down-
stairs loo.'

'That's why the interior décor is my department, dear,' said Emily, standing up. 'Oh, by the way. What was it that you and your pals were discussing so avidly in the garden yesterday?'

Oscar Mansfield paused, uncertain how to deal with this question. He didn't know whether the prospective partners would be telling their wives about the idea. The cautionary note struck by Mr La Fontayne about the interests of the families had raised doubts in his mind about how the women would react to the news that others were benefiting from their husbands' deaths.

But there was no possibility of deceiving Emily. Most of the time she knew what he thought before he had actually thought it. And there was another more attractive side to his grand idea: the wives would indeed be the beneficiaries, so long as it was one of the other three husbands who had died.

'Life insurance,' he said.

'Life insurance?' said Emily. 'It all looked a lot more interesting than that.'

'Yes, it was,' he agreed. 'Do you want to hear about it?'

She put down the cups that she was about to transfer to the kitchen and sat down again. 'Tell me,' she said.

Oscar Mansfield outlined his plan, worried about how she would react. Her eyebrows, raised at first in quizzical interest, descended slowly during his exposition to comprise at the end a disapproving frown.

37

'A typical male idea, if I may say so,' she said when he had finished. 'I can't imagine a woman cooking up an idea like that.'

'But the women will benefit, too,' said Oscar. 'Two wives will benefit twice and the last one four times if she outlives her husband — which women usually do.'

Emily stood up. 'Oscar, I find this somewhat morbid. That's what I meant by a male idea.'

'The beauty of it is,' said Oscar, starting at last to help with the clearing up, 'it encourages wives to look after their husbands and ensure that they stay in good health. The right diet, no stress, loving care and attention.'

'And what do the other wives think about it?'

'I haven't heard that yet,' Oscar admitted. 'I expect Lavinia Wyatt will be quite enthusiastic. Her husband jogs and goes to gyms. That lovely head of blond hair — he'll live for ever.' He gazed morosely in the kitchen mirror at his own premature baldness.

'It's not what's on your head that counts, it's what's in it,' said Emily briskly. 'I wouldn't call Julian Wyatt's mind well-furnished. I can't imagine him going to bed with Alexis de Tocqueville or Søren Kierkegaard.'

'I should hope not,' said Oscar. 'Lavinia would be cross.'

'And there's something fundamentally nondescript about Vernon Jones. He always looks so depressed.'

'Depressed? He's suicidal.'

'But neither looks as old as you! I bet they're both laughing their socks off now at the very idea that it should have been you who came up with this daft scheme.'

But what Vernon Jones and Julian Wyatt are actually doing at this moment is trying to earn a living.

At the college where Jones lectures, an atmosphere of moral decay permeates the flagstone corridor and the dank yellow-walled classrooms. He sees himself as a man who is fighting a battle that is already lost, but not yet over; the defeat is clear but the struggle has to go on.

In a room that would hold many more, he is talking this morning with a dozen sixteen and seventeen-year-olds about America's contribution to the English language, about how they took it and tweaked it, but he can see before he is in his stride that his audience is too familiar with a transatlantic way with words to recognise the English origins. He has long since lost all respect for the youngsters who confront him here. They seem to him to be vulgar, anarchic, sullen and combative, and these are just the promising ones who might go on to a red-brick university in some godforsaken corner of the island.

He stands before them at a lectern on which his well-thumbed notes lie in no particular order. The students lounge around the room as if they are relaxing in a fast-food establishment, only occasionally appearing to give him the favour of their attention.

'America's contribution to the English language goes back much further than you might suppose,' he tells them. 'When you think of Americanisms you probably think of stuff you hear on television every night, but the fact is that we were gratefully accepting their words more than a hundred years ago, their words and their phrases. Can anybody think of any?'

Inviting a response from these people is a risky venture. It too easily emphasises their lack of interest in what he has been saying, and he looks at them with a hostility that is balefully returned. Rosemary Friedland repeatedly uses both hands to adjust a bow at the back of her head, a gesture which satisfactorily disposes of any doubts about the generous dimensions of her breasts. Jones remembers that when he was her age he thought that touching a girl's breasts would land him in court, and his eyes linger on her, hoping that she might provide an answer that will allow him to give her his full attention. She has the face of an angel but the shoulders of a swimmer. Middle-aged men, he reflects, have always been attracted to teenage girls. The only thing that has stopped many of them from making fools of themselves is the quality of the conversation they would have to endure.

'I'll tell you some,' he says, transferring his attention to Richard Pritchard and Walter Boulter. It is an irony not lost on Jones that this troublesome couple with their rhyming names have a maladroit touch with verse. 'To face the music, to bark up the wrong tree, to have a chip on your shoulder, to pull the wool over your eyes, to knuckle down, even to have a stiff upper lip are all Americanisms which we have gladly accepted.'

These facts, fascinating to Jones, are met with a wall of apathy that he ignores.

'And words,' he says. 'Where would we be without the help of our American cousins? Commuter, hangover, fountain pen, escalator. It wasn't the English who dreamed that quartet up.'

The lecturer pauses and glances at his class. Sometimes it is difficult to tell why they are here when they would quite clearly prefer to be elsewhere. Pritchard, particularly, is not even feigning the interest which other students deem necessary and is drawing what appears to be a naked woman on the back of his folder.

'They even have words for you, Pritchard,' says Jones. 'Moron and deadbeat are two of them.'

Pritchard can no longer display disinterest in the face of this open attack. He puts down his pen and says: 'Sometimes I think you pick on me, Mr Jones.'

Jones looks at Pritchard, with his bizarre haircut and permanent cagoule. He always seems to have a suntan which Jones regards as the sign of a frivolous person.

'Pick on you?' he asks.

'Yes, you mark me down. You gave me twenty for punctuation when the others were in the sixties. I know what a comma is. I even know how to use a semi-colon.'

A vindictive smile dawns on Jones's face.

'Let's try you, Pritchard. I'll dictate one sentence to you and if you can punctuate it correctly I'll go down on my knees and apologise.'

The prospect of an act of abasement from Mr Jones, a figure he cordially loathes, brings a smile to Pritchard's face too, and he produces a sheet of paper from his folder.

'Shoot,' he says.

'Smith where Brown,' says Jones.

'Which where is that?' asks Pritchard.

'Work it out from the sentence,' says Jones. 'Now write the word "had" eleven times.'

Pritchard scowls and writes.

'Got it?' asks Jones, and Pritchard nods. 'The examiner's approval.'

'Is that it?' asks Pritchard.

'That's it,' says Jones. 'Now punctuate it.'

This diversion has halted the lesson. Other students have written down the sentence too and are pondering eleven consecutive 'hads'. Jones returns to his lectern and gathers his notes. There are another ten minutes here and he has not quite finished. This afternoon there is a cricket match which means that this day, at least, hasn't been entirely wasted. His real ambition is to turn his leg break.

He goes on: 'On the other hand there are some words that we think are American but actually originated here. They fell into disuse in Britain but were resurrected over there. Does anybody know of any?'

Once again his question is met by a ghastly silence.

'The punctuation is for Pritchard, not the rest of you,' he says, and a few students put down their pens. 'Fall, which the Americans prefer to autumn, is actually Old English and was much used here in the last century. If it wasn't for America it would have mysteriously died out.'

'That's interesting,' says a studious girl at the front of the class who wears enormous spectacles and is called Felicity Fisher. 'But why do the Americans spell words differently, like theatre and favour, and pronounce some words differently as well, like lieutenant?'

'That's a topic I shall be returning to,' says Jones, who doesn't know the answer. 'We're running out of time. How's the punctuation coming along, Pritchard?'

'I can't make sense of it,' says Pritchard. 'It's not a sentence at all.'

'It will be a sentence when you've punctuated it,' says Jones. 'That's what punctuation is for, to make sense out of words.'

'Well, I can't do it.'

'Can anybody?' asks Jones.

Again he is confronted by twelve faces without an answer, and he picks up a crayon and goes to the white board at the front of the room. When he was at school the board was black.

'The answer is this,' he says, and writes on the board: *Smith, where Brown had had 'had', had had 'had had'; 'had had' had had the examiner's approval.* He turns to Pritchard. 'Punctuation makes sense of words.'

43

'Donnez-moi un break,' says Pritchard.

At the office where Julian Wyatt struggles daily for professional survival, his staff are carried along on a wave of enthusiasm, buoyed up by the frenetic bustle around them, as if the recession can be defeated by application, inspiration and hard work. In one corner a bearded young man is designing the label for a can of peas, in another a young woman in her twenties is producing on-screen a brochure for a small group of hotels. The advertising director is showing a potential client the facilities they have at their disposal and samples of the work they have produced. Another man talks earnestly on the phone to the marketing manager of a leisure group who are planning a holiday village with log cabins, badger trails and a lake, and might at some stage be persuaded to divert a minuscule portion of their £100 million budget to the depleted coffers of Wyatt Promotions.

Divorced from this creative activity, Julian Wyatt sits in a small office at one end of the floor, separated from his staff by temporary walls of hardboard that don't quite reach the ceiling. There has never been either the time or the money to finish this office to his satisfaction, but he sits in this makeshift corner working his way through a list of telephone calls that he must make. His present one is to the VAT men who want £10,000 today. The fact that Julian Wyatt has not yet received the money on which this amount will be owed presents a serious obstacle to his writing the cheque for which the taxmen are now clamouring, and he is engaged now in a humbling negotiation for payments by instalment, an offer that is only accepted with the proviso that a substantial bill for interest will be added to the debt. His next call is to the financial director of a toys and games conglomerate who are proving characteristically sluggish in settling an account. Where once there was the single challenge of earning some money, he now every day confronts two: first he must earn it, then he must get his increasingly desperate hands on the cheque. Reluctance to pay is a disease that spreads, contaminating respectable institutions whose profits and viability are not in question. Hanging on to the money for a month or two, and thus getting the interest out of it, has become not only a way of life but a factor in the balance sheets and for Julian Wyatt, who has no balance to speak of, it means further imploratory phone calls, at first to the firm in question and then, blocked by bureaucrats, to his banks.

The tightrope that he walks creates a pressure that affects both his personality and his appearance. Patience and a sense of humour have long gone, and his face, if not haggard, is beginning to look slightly pinched. To a man of Julian Wyatt's vanity these are serious matters, and the jogging and the gym visits are partly designed to restore the glow of youthful health that his professional life seems determined to erase.

That evening in Gerry's Gym, as he pedals ferociously on a Schwinn Airdyne exercise bike, he wonders

45

whether his exhausting ordeal is making him younger or older. A little screen near the handlebars that move with his efforts so that he is exercising his arms as well as his legs, tells him that he is burning off 400 calories an hour.

Gerry, the slim middle-aged man who presides over this temple of health in a subfusc tracksuit, tells him: 'The more efficient the heart gets the slower it beats. The average is seventy-two, mine is sixty, Gordon Pirie's was forty. Yours will soon be around sixty.'

Gerry has devised a routine of exercises for Julian Wyatt, based on his lifestyle and what he is trying to achieve. Most visitors to his gym are there to lose weight and many are women, but Julian Wyatt's objective seems to be to attain a standard of fitness that will push the ageing process into the next century or beyond.

He jumps from the bike and moves to the chest-exercise machine where he hauls huge weights from behind each shoulder. Nearby an older man is running on the jogging machine which he has raised at one end so that he runs uphill. None of the people here seem to have enough breath left to talk to the others.

On the bench press Julian Wyatt lies on his back and pushes up 35 kilograms twenty times, and then he moves to the sit-up bench, pulling himself up repeatedly while his feet are tucked under a retaining bar.

'What's my life expectancy, Gerry?' he asks when he has completed his programme. 'I'm getting insured.'

'For men these days it's seventy-two,' says Gerry. 'Twenty years ago it was sixty-eight.'

'You mean they're living longer anyway, without going through this hell?'

'Seventy-two is the average,' says Gerry. 'You'll see eighty unless a brick falls on your head.'

'What happened to Gordon Pirie?'

'He died, unfortunately.'

'I thought all this exercise prolonged active life, like the dog food?'

'Well,' says Gerry, 'it's not written in stone.'

In the Oasis of Sanity Julian Wyatt eschews his customary orange juice and opts for a pint of Old Peculiar. The link between extraordinary fitness and triumphant longevity seems less certain than he had believed.

'Alcohol already!' says Oscar Mansfield, ensconced like a permanent fixture at the end of the counter. 'Joy shall be in Heaven over one sinner that repenteth.'

'I was thinking of going on a stress-management course, but alcohol is cheaper,' says Julian Wyatt.

'Very wise of you. There's no such thing as a tense alcoholic, hence the expression "relaxed as a newt".'

Colin Dunbar interrupts these banalities by placing a sheet of paper on the bar.

'There it is,' he says. 'A message from my doctor. He says no finer figure ever graced his surgery. If everybody was like me the medical profession would be facing starvation.'

'Good man, Colin,' says Oscar Mansfield, studying

47

the document. 'What about you, Julian? A medical attendance report is what we need.'

'What about a deposition from Gerry's Gym? He says I'll live to be eighty.'

'The insurance people prefer to take the word of a medical gentleman, not some shifty muscle man who's ripping off fat ladies.'

'I'll fix it,' says Julian Wyatt. 'This beer's rather good. I think I'll have another.'

His newly-filled glass is handed across to him as the door opens and Jones comes in. He is wearing the white flannels of a cricketer and the sun has reddened his face.

'My God,' says Colin. 'Another get-fit fanatic. We don't want you fit, kid, we just want you insured.'

Jones puts some money on the counter and asks for a lager. A notice on the oak beam over his head says DUCK OR GROUSE.

'You're not all still pursuing Oscar's crazy idea, are you?' he asks. 'I thought you'd all forget it by now.'

'We're on,' says Julian. 'Are you?'

'Why should I?' says Jones. 'Remind me.'

'Jesus, Jones,' says Julian. 'I can see why you're not Master of Balliol.'

'Listen, Vernon,' says Oscar Mansfield soothingly, 'if you come in, there are four possibilities for you – just four. One is that you die, in which case nothing matters. Two, you get £33,000. Three, you get £83,000 and four, you get £183,000.'

'Put like that, you'd better include me in,' says Jones.

48

'Go for it, Oscar,' says Colin. 'Get this lot in line.'

Oscar picks up his beer. 'I'll have it all ready by the weekend. Join Oscar's little scheme! Everyone's a winner! Well, nearly everyone.'

4

The home to which Julian Wyatt swayed half an hour later was a detached period house with a walled garden, six bedrooms and a large conservatory where on summer evenings Lavinia liked to serve dinner. Twelve years ago when their son Gavin was born, Julian had bought the place for £50,000 and hoped that it was now worth six times as much, because he used it as security against part of his bank loans.

Lavinia Wyatt was a beautiful, slim blonde of thirty-six, although this was not an age she would admit to. The damning evidence provided by a son of twelve was mitigated somewhat by her frequent assertions that she had given birth at eighteen. She was a woman whom many men found attractive and she did nothing to discourage them. With her son at boarding school and her husband away for eleven hours a day there were spaces and gaps in her life that she needed to fill. Tonight she greeted her husband in a tight white dress that stopped well above the knee, and gave him a chaste kiss on the cheek.

'Have you been drinking?' she asked, surprised.

Julian Wyatt slumped into a bamboo chair in the conservatory and agreed that he had.

'But you don't drink.'

'It's not written in stone,' he said, drunkenly reiterating what Gerry had said to him in the gym. 'I haven't signed any pledge.'

'Well, I've seen you drink champagne occasionally, but that doesn't smell like champagne.'

'Old Peculiar,' said Julian Wyatt. 'It's a bitter that a lot of people drink.'

'And what about the fitness programme? You're on orange juice and exercise, not pints of bloody beer.'

Julian Wyatt stood up. 'We're going to hell in a handcart, darling. I need some consolations. When's dinner? I want a shower first.'

Twenty minutes later, washed, refreshed and dressed in jeans and a yellow short-sleeve shirt, he joined his wife for a dinner of roast beef in the conservatory. On the floor beside them the cat was clearing a saucer of lumpfish caviar.

'What do you mean,' asked Lavinia, pouring herself a glass of chablis and her husband some Evian water, 'going to hell in a handcart?'

'It's an expression.'

'I know it's an expression, but how does it apply to us?'

Julian Wyatt glanced down at the cat and its

expensive supper and tried not to think about Lavinia's extravagance. She could go into a store merely to escape the rain and come out with goods that cost several hundred pounds. He, on the other hand, was more careful with his money, always intending but never quite managing to do next year's Christmas shopping in the January sales. You went into shops because you needed to buy something, not in the hope that you would find something that you hadn't realised you wanted.

'It applies to us like this,' he said. 'I don't repay my loans. I "renegotiate" them. The banks are beginning to communicate on a day-to-day basis, my clients are among the slowest payers in the world, I'm employing salesmen who couldn't sell a drink to a thirsty millionaire, and those parts of my little empire that do make money are quite unintentionally bringing us to our knees because by some strange quirk of the financial world the more money we make the more money we need to borrow.'

Lavinia Wyatt's comminatory tone faded a little in the face of this gloomy synopsis. 'That doesn't make sense to me,' she said irritably.

'It doesn't make sense to me either, but not much does these days. It's all to do with borrowing money to finance business that will eventually make money.'

'Why don't you finance the business with money you have made?'

'Because it's all paying off the debts that paid for earlier work. Anybody who borrowed to set up a business in the last few years is in it up to here. And I did.'

He concentrated on his roast beef while his wife mulled this over. Casualties of the recession had become too numerous for her to dismiss it all as one of Julian's moods. People were selling their houses and looking for somewhere smaller. There were fewer Range Rovers about. Holiday destinations, if they existed at all, were nearer and cheaper. And Gavin had written this morning from Somerset to say that two of his best friends had left because their parents could no longer pay the school fees. The prospect of Gavin suffering a similar fate filled her with horror.

'Julian, this is appalling,' she said. Words like economy, sacrifice and thrift ran through her head. They were not words that she had ever liked or used, and she dismissed them immediately like a maiden aunt who has overheard talk of sex. 'What are we going to do?'

'Kiss the bank managers' boots and battle on. I'm in a nasty little loop at the moment, working this month to pay for the work I did last month. Is there any beer in this house?'

'Beer?' said Lavinia with alarm. 'We've never had beer in this house.'

'That might have been one of our mistakes. It turns out that beer is cheaper than champagne.'

'Corned beef is cheaper than fillet steak but I've never heard you suggest that we buy some.'

'Needs must, kid. Corned beef and beer. Christ!'

Lavinia Wyatt pushed the rest of her dinner away and reached for the wine. 'Why don't you sell it?' she asked. 'Let someone else do the struggling and get some capital you can use on another venture.'

'Sell what?'

'Wyatt Promotions.'

'Sell it? I'd have to pay somebody to take it off my hands.'

With this demoralising thought he pushed his own food away and filled his glass with water. The beer had spoiled his appetite but left him with a thirst. His wife looked at the abandoned meal and drank her wine, but the sombre tone of her husband's conversations raised doubts that no amount of chablis would subdue.

Later, when they shared the sofa in front of the television and tried to become involved in the puerile antics of a game show, he said: 'I'm seeing a doctor tomorrow.'

She turned from the television to look at him. If there was more bad news on the way she was not sure that she could take it.

'What about?'

'Oscar Mansfield has had this rather amusing idea that involves four of us insuring our lives. I need a report from the doctor to say I'm okay.'

'I'm not sure that I approve of this idea, Julian,' she said when the scheme had been explained to her. 'If you were to pass away I rather thought that I'd be the person to benefit financially.'

'To cushion you in your moments of sorrow, do you mean?' he asked, laughing. 'There's a policy that will give you and Gavin a quarter of a million straight away if I die in the next ten years. This is just a joke thing costing a hundred a month.'

'Well, that's four bottles of champagne for a start,' said Lavinia.

'But we've got three chances out of four of benefiting from it. If one of the others dies first the money flows in, and Jones never stops talking about topping himself which we all find very encouraging. He says that four out of every five suicides are men. They're disembowelling themselves with bread-knives in the back garden these days, apparently. When was the last time you heard of a housewife committing suicide?'

Lavinia Wyatt shook her head in disbelief.

'Men are extraordinary creatures,' she said. 'We're going to depend for our financial salvation on a friend killing himself, are we?'

'Not necessarily. There are road accidents and heart attacks and air crashes. Do you know the most dangerous sport in Britain? Angling. They drown at an amazing rate. Forty-two deaths in the last four years. Only thirteen died motor racing.'

'None of your friends fish, do they?'

'I'm going to buy them some rods,' said Julian Wyatt.

Jones lived in a detached four-bedroom bungalow that had among its additional attractions a greenhouse and a potting shed, two havens he increasingly retreated to when the need for solitude became overwhelming. Between the hostility of his students and the antipathy of his wife, his appetite for seclusion grew, and he now spent more time watching tomatoes than he did television.

He had met Gaynor when she was a student of eighteen and he, ten years older, was a lecturer with a future. It seemed to her then that he knew everything there was to know and, admiring his wisdom and his knowledge, she set about winning him. They married when he was thirty and she was twenty but now, fifteen years later, the gap in their ages had miraculously expanded to far more than a mere decade. At thirty-five she still felt as if she was in her twenties, but Jones at forty-five had the appearance and attitudes of a man of fifty. It was an additional grouse of Gaynor's that no children had appeared despite a rumbustious sex-life in the early days; the prospect of her offspring inheriting the brainpower of a lecturer had been a powerful motive in her quest for him.

Today, disillusioned and thwarted, she found herself saddled with a miserable old man whose life was a dreary treadmill and whose hopes for the future, fiercely ambitious at twenty-eight, had been comprehensively quashed. She used her time reading books and playing tennis, but mostly she just liked to get out of the home. Films, art exhibitions, garden centres or even churches beckoned her out into the world where she forgot about the four-bedroom bungalow and dreamed of flight.

Tonight, in a short blue skirt and a pink turtleneck sweater, she did indeed look nearer twenty than forty. Her dark, curly hair ringed a serious girlish face untouched by the rigours of child-rearing or a demanding career. When Jones arrived in his cricket gear, clutching a batch of students' essays, she had already eaten and was curled up on the sofa with a book on patronage in Renaissance Italy.

'There's a fish pie you can put in the microwave,' she told him without looking up. Separate meals seemed to epitomise his life, he thought, and wondered not for the first time why she couldn't wait to eat with him. He went into the bedroom to change, emerged in slacks and an old blue shirt, and then went into the kitchen to heat the fish pie. He looked round for something to drink with it; a jeroboam of cleaning fluid would have suited his mood. He ate in the kitchen alone, drinking a can of beer that he found at the back of the fridge, and then wandered into the sitting room where his wife was still reading.

He took the armchair opposite her and picked up his pile of essays. The subject he had set, *Are fathers just a wallet?*, did not promise an enlightening half hour, and the first effort he picked up suggested that the class hadn't even begun to think seriously about the subject.

Gaynor Jones, bored by her book, finally looked up. 'I've been thinking,' she said, smiling for once.

'About what?' asked Jones, laying down his essays. He wondered whether trying to track her unpredictable moodshifts was damaging his brain.

'Why don't we ever invite anyone round for dinner?'

Jones looked at her, wondering who she had in mind. He had to be careful what he promised after a few drinks. Sober, he was often far from enthusiastic about what he had committed himself to.

'You know I don't like visitors here,' he suggested.

'You don't want them to see the crappy state of the carpets.'

'I don't give a sod what they think of the carpets. When have I ever cared about what people think? It's that you can't get rid of them when you want to. It's not the host who decides when they go. The visitor decides and you're their bloody slave.' He leaned forward in his chair and mimed the role. 'Can I get you another drink? Would you like a coffee? Are you hungry? Do you need a woman with big breasts? Haven't you got a bloody home to go to?'

Gaynor Jones watched this display with her customary dispassion. 'Are you neurotic or psychotic?' she asked.

'Robotic,' said Jones. 'Trained to do the same thing every day. If you want to have dinner with someone we'll take them to a restaurant. That way you can quit when you want to.'

'That isn't the same thing at all.'

'It sounds near enough to me. Whom did you want to invite?'

'It doesn't matter who I want to invite. It's just the idea of actually having guests in this place, of having a social life. It's what people do.'

'Well, I don't know anybody who does it. Nobody ever invites me round for dinner.'

'Are you surprised? It'd be like inviting Dracula to a christening.'

It was at moments like this that Jones retreated to the orderly calm of the potting shed, but tonight he had essays to read and mark and he was obliged to stay in the room.

For Gaynor Jones, her husband's reluctance to have guests was just one more addition to her complaints about him. It was a long list that began with the comparatively trivial — cigarette ash strewn carelessly throughout the bungalow, leaves and grass thought-lessly transferred from the garden to the carpets, flecks of meat on the bathroom mirror, catapulted from between his teeth by the magic of Dental Floss — and moved on to more serious complaints about sex and money that, she increasingly felt, only divorce would remedy.

'I'm going to bed,' she announced, and she left without waiting for a reply.

Jones would like to have gone to bed as well. The worse his life became the more he welcomed sleep. Something which he had once delayed as long as possible now provided the peace and oblivion for which he longed.

He picked up the essays again and started to read. It was clearly a subject that had aroused more interest among the girls than the boys, who appeared to have seldom given their fathers a thought.

Felicity Fisher was anxious to prove that fathers were only a wallet, but wanted to explain and forgive. *Fathers are semi-detached*, she wrote, *removed from everyday family life by a combination of circumstances that range from the economic to the biological. They spend most of their waking hours away from home, earning the money to pay for it. Nature has programmed them to procreate but not to wash up, and to that extent they are not a domestic animal at all. They keep their distance and complain a lot and it is hard not to feel sorry for them. But the fact is that in the end a wallet is all they are, and the tragedy is that a wallet is all they aspire to be.*

Jones found this essay so depressing that he wished he had given his students a different subject to write about.

Rosemary Friedland, that most attractive of the creatures who listened or pretended to listen to his talks, seemed obsessed by the fact that men had external sex organs, as if this somehow excused them from having normal human responses. *To men, a liaison with the opposite sex is a sort of extra-curricular activity that has no place in the mainstream of their lives*, she wrote. *For most of the time their interests lie elsewhere, like a male animal in the wild.*

Jones didn't feel like a male animal in the wild; he felt like a captive in one of the harsher European zoos. He wrote at the bottom of Felicity Fisher's essay: *Empathetic and yet detached and ironic,* and wondered what he was doing fostering the aspirations of a group

61

of youngsters who sadly despised him. He read the essays with a sinking heart, and then finished his beer and headed for the conjugal bed.

Although nobody who knew him would take the idea seriously, what he really needed, mentally, spiritually and physically, he knew, was a stupendous bout of extra-marital sex.

5

In a spirit of cautious optimism Oscar Mansfield assembled the ingredients of his inaugural barbecue and transferred them with loving care from the kitchen to the patio. Chicken breasts, steaks, spare ribs, chops, sausages, hamburgers, Portuguese sardines and Mediterranean king prawns were carried out first, followed by new potatoes that Emily had already cooked, lettuce, tomatoes, courgettes, onions, mushrooms and sweetcorn. Skewered bananas and kebabs of peppers, tomatoes and mushrooms came next, along with a fruit punch that he had made from red wine, vodka and limejuice.

But first he had to light the barbecue, a task which proved to be more difficult than he had expected. He arranged his charcoal briquettes in an elegant ziggurat, festooned with Zip firelighters, sprinkled them both with white spirit and struck a match. The trouble he had in getting it to catch raised his opinion of arsonists, wrestling with their lonely and impossibly demanding trade, but finally there was fire, and he went off to get a glass of punch before the guests arrived.

The party on this Sunday afternoon was to celebrate the completion of Oscar's grand insurance idea. The medical reports had been received, the insurance policies were in place, the Trust was set up and each member had arranged his standing order at the bank. There was nothing more to be done.

Obtaining the medical documents that the insurance company wanted had been a straightforward matter for three of them, but Jones's doctor, confronted by an enervated forty-five-year-old smoker, felt that the situation called for something more than the usual cursory inspection, and had embarked on a series of tests on his patient's heart, blood, lungs, hearing, height and weight, which satisfied the doctor but greatly alarmed Jones. When he heard of the ease with which the others had acquired their medical reports, he felt singled out, and began to wonder whether his doctor had spotted something that he was too kind to mention. He imagined the ailments that had queued up to invade his body and had to remind himself repeatedly that the doctor had in the end produced a report which assured whomever it may concern that Jones was fit and eminently insurable.

The other smoker, today's host, evidently enjoyed a personal friendship with his doctor who would have signed whatever Oscar put before him. But Oscar was five years younger than Jones and, removed from the trials and tribulations of trying to earn a living, was so relaxed that it was difficult for his doctor to determine sometimes how he managed to stay awake for a whole day.

'You're losing your hair and you drink too much, Oscar, but you already know that,' he had said. 'Have you ever considered doing a little exercise?'

'My angle on that is that if you're fit you don't need it, and if you're not you shouldn't take it.'

'You'll live to be a hundred, Oscar.'

'I hope so,' said Oscar. 'I have every incentive.'

Julian Wyatt's own doctor, who hadn't seen him since an ear-syringing appointment five years earlier, was surprised by his appearance.

'What on earth have you been up to, Mr Wyatt?' he asked. 'You've aged ten years in five.'

'Working and jogging,' said Julian.

'There's a couple of activities that put years on you,' said the doctor. 'I'd try to get some relaxation in your life, if I were you.'

'Fat chance,' said Julian. 'Do you find anything to alarm an insurance company?'

'They'll love you,' said the doctor, lighting a cigarette. 'They love joggers.'

Colin Dunbar had submitted himself to an exhaustive medical when he took out a mortgage on the Oasis of Sanity, and the documents he required for the insurance company were forwarded to him without seeing a doctor. The Dunbars had shut their bar restaurant with unconcealed relief to enjoy the rare pleasure of eating and drinking on someone else's premises.

'It's so strange to see you in your own environment, Oscar,' said Fay. 'I've only known you propped up at the end of the bar. Now I discover you can stand up and do things.'

Fay Dunbar was wearing a white off-the-shoulder dress that made her look younger than thirty while simultaneously making Oscar feel much older than forty.

'My husband has many talents,' Emily Mansfield told her, 'when his mind isn't impaired by the mists and vapours of alcohol. He even built this barbecue.'

Fay Dunbar studied it admiringly. 'Colin is less capable. He built a bird-table once that toppled over when a sparrow landed on it.'

The Wyatts arrived in their deep green Range Rover that had been bought through the firm which paid for its fuel and upkeep. It was used almost exclusively by Lavinia for her shopping and social engagements. When her husband wasn't jogging, he travelled by taxi and train.

'Come over here and give me a sample of your conversation,' said Oscar Mansfield, who was always pleased to see Lavinia Wyatt. 'I'm going to make much of you.'

Lavinia was wearing a red lace-knit dress with a bolero jacket, and looked as if she had strayed from one of the Sunday magazines.

'What is this crazy scheme you have dreamed up, Oscar?' she asked. 'Are you waiting for my husband to die?'

'Only if it will bring us closer,' said Oscar, pouring

fruit punch into two goblets. 'We can't wait until I lose my libido, hair and teeth.'

'You still have all those, darling, do you?' asked his wife, who was now laying a large white table on the patio. 'Look in the mirror.'

'It's not my libido she's talking about then,' said Oscar, winking lasciviously. 'Ah, here come Mr and Mrs Jones.'

Vernon and Gaynor Jones had arrived at Rose Cottage on foot and came round the side of the house now with the restrained smiles of reluctant guests. Jones, ill at ease in these situations, still had the Sunday newspapers to read, and Gaynor's social pleasures were greatly enhanced if they were conducted in the absence of her neurasthenic spouse.

'You can cheer up now, Jones,' said Julian Wyatt. 'The doctor has told you that there is nothing to worry about.'

Jones nodded and smiled, feeling that it would be impolite to challenge the veracity of this. At the last count the only trivialities that were left for him to worry about were inflation, interest rates, the ozone layer, the weather, the Health Service, crime in the streets, pollution in the air, danger on the roads, sewage on the beaches, sinister dictators stockpiling nuclear weapons, and the lazy incompetence of almost everybody he had to deal with, including his wife.

'Everything's fine,' he said. 'Thanks for the invitation, Oscar.'

'We trustees must stick together,' said Oscar, handing

the newcomers fruit punch. 'I hope you brought your appetite with you.' The charcoal now glowed red and managed from its small shelf to add to the heat of the day. Emily Mansfield laid grey translucent prawns on the grill and Jones watched as they became orangey-pink.

'I saw your letter in the paper, Emily,' he said. 'In fact, I've seen several.'

'It's a way of letting off steam, Vernon,' she told him. 'I've got a couple more to write when I get a moment. Perhaps, with all that education, you can straighten me out on one of them. Why do people starve in Africa while farmers in Europe are paid a fortune not to grow food?'

'I imagine it's a logistical problem,' said Jones.

'We can get a man to the moon but we can't get bread to Africa?'

'They don't eat bread, do they? They eat maize.'

'Well, we could grow maize, couldn't we? We could send eggs.'

'Eggs don't travel that well, I believe.'

'Sainsbury's seem to manage it,' said Emily Mansfield briskly. 'And here's another one. Why do we send people to prison for ten years and let them out after five if they're good, when everybody else sends them to prison for ten years and lets them out after fifteen if they're bad?'

'My God, Emily,' said Jones. 'Does your brain ever rest?'

'I should hope not,' she said, carrying the prawns

across to the table where a quite different conversation was in progress.

'About the only thing it's still illegal to show on television is an erect penis,' Lavinia Wyatt informed the guests with lubricious glee.

'Even if they could find one in these depressed times,' said Gaynor Jones.

This gap in their viewing material, now that it had been pointed out, produced a rapt silence which only their host could break.

'Why do you want to see an erect penis on television?' asked Oscar. 'I know the little box is a substitute life for soap-opera addicts, but you deserve the real, three-dimensional business. Here's my number.'

'I didn't say I wanted to see one,' said Lavinia Wyatt. 'God forbid! I was merely drawing attention to the prohibition.'

More food arrived: sausages, chicken breasts, chops and steaks. Soon Emily Mansfield was able to abandon the barbecue and join them to eat at the table.

'No vegetarians here, I hope?' she asked, and receiving no answer continued to chat while she sliced up a sausage. 'I don't understand these dietary fads. Animals eat animals: it's a law of nature. The only thing that matters is a humane form of slaughter. The Jews hang live animals upside down and slit their throats to conform to their barmy ideas about food.'

'Oh dear, Oscar,' said Gaynor Jones. 'I think you've married an anti-Semite.'

'Let me put you right, dear,' said Emily Mansfield

between mouthfuls. 'I don't like the Jews in the same way that I don't like the Protestants or the Catholics or the Methodists or the Muslims or any of the other madmen who think they're going to survive the crematorium and want to convey this ludicrous belief to the rest of us — with explosives if necessary. The whole lot of them represent a malignant cancer in the human race.'

'Well, that's religion taken care of,' beamed Oscar Mansfield. 'Any other ideas you want to unburden yourself of, darling?'

'I think I can feel another letter coming on,' said Jones.

'Well, I'm right, aren't I?' demanded Emily. 'Behind every street bomb for the last forty years there's been a religion. Check it.'

'Your word's good enough for me,' said Julian Wyatt. 'I ditched God and Father Christmas the same year. My life didn't suffer at all, although the presents dropped off a bit.' He was about to say more about this when a plaintive whine rose from his blazer pocket.

'Not that bloody phone again,' said Oscar Mansfield. 'I meant to ban it from the garden.'

'Well, what the hell do you think I pay you for?' said Julian Wyatt into his mobile phone, but then, sensing the disapproval of the others, he stood up and left the table to continue his call at the end of the garden.

Fay Dunbar, less at home here than the others, said: 'They ring him in the bar sometimes. He never seems to get a happy phone call. I don't know why he carries the thing.'

'No pain, no gain,' said Lavinia Wyatt. 'My husband's running an empire. It's not supposed to be easy.'

Oscar Mansfield had taken advantage of the interruption to produce some spare ribs and kebabs and soon the plates that were rapidly being cleared were covered with food again, while Julian Wyatt remonstrated into his mobile phone beside the beech hedge at the end of the lawn.

'We should hire these people to do our cooking,' said Colin Dunbar. 'They're getting a flavour here that we can't match.'

'How is the Oasis of Sanity, anyway?' asked Emily. 'I keep meaning to eat there.'

'I wish somebody would,' said Colin. 'Eating out seems to have been struck off the list of leisure activities.'

Julian Wyatt switched off his phone and tramped across the lawn looking like a man who had just taken part in a deeply unwelcome conversation with his doctor. He slumped in his chair and stared with no interest at the spare ribs.

'How are you all feeling?' he asked the men. 'I think I need a windfall from the insurance scheme.'

'After a feast like this?' said Jones. 'Never better.' There seemed to be enough food between his teeth to keep him going for a couple of days if he didn't use his Dental Floss.

'I'm afraid I don't get ill, either,' said Oscar. 'Since I stopped mixing with the public I don't even have colds. You get crowds, you get germs.'

'Falderal, Oscar!' said his wife. 'The sun's cooked his brains. It's mixing with the germ-ridden public that keeps your immunity system in shape.'

'Bad news again, darling?' asked Lavinia Wyatt.

'What other sort is there?' asked her husband. 'I'm beginning to wish I had a normal job with a regular salary cheque at the end of the month.'

'You had a normal job but the firm collapsed on top of you, if you remember. You're self-employed because no one else will employ you.'

'Thank you, darling,' said Julian Wyatt, gritting his teeth.

'I'll employ you,' said Colin Dunbar. 'Fill the Oasis of Sanity with hungry crowds clutching pretty credit cards. I'm talking starving multitudes here.'

'I could do that quite easily, but would you like my bill?'

'Are you expensive?' asked Fay Dunbar.

'Ruinously,' said Julian Wyatt, 'but as nobody pays their debts these days it doesn't discourage clients.'

Hot skewered bananas, rolled in sugar, appeared on the table, and Oscar Mansfield refilled the glasses with punch. He wondered whether to suggest a little croquet, but his guests seemed so comfortable and satisfied that he decided it would be a disruption.

Jones sat back in his chair, legs crossed, feeling an unaccustomed mood of conviviality. A reluctantly accepted invitation had produced a wonderfully relaxing interlude, and his spirits had been vastly improved by the distressed remarks of his self-employed friends who obviously lived in a daily nightmare of unsympathetic balance sheets and inadequate custom. The structured wage slavery which he knew to be his lot seemed, in this tormented company, to be an enviable option instead of the pauper's manacle he had always thought it.

Julian Wyatt stared at the Mansfields' immaculate lawn, his feet tapping restlessly. This peaceful rural setting made the ill-humoured bedlam of his office seem worse than it was because it emphasised the gulf that existed between his life and the life of people like Oscar Mansfield who passed their days with hover mowers and peat-free composts and received no angry phone calls at all, let alone those that made your heart beat faster and no doubt shortened your life — an important consideration now that he had signed Oscar's papers.

'Any requests?' asked their busy hostess.

'Yes,' said Julian Wyatt. 'Don't let tomorrow come.'

Oscar Mansfield, feeling the need to dispel this depression, produced a bottle of wine from the kitchen.

'My fellow trustees, I would like you all to mark the establishment of our Trust by drinking a toast to a long and happy life,' he said.

'That's a bit of a paradox, isn't it?' said his wife. 'Verging on the oxymoronic.'

'Well, moronic, anyway,' said Lavinia Wyatt. 'Are you sure this toast is sincere?'

'Sancerre, actually,' said Oscar, looking at the label. He filled the wine glasses and handed them round.

'Here's to us,' said Colin Dunbar.

'May you all live for ever and enrich the insurance company,' said Emily Mansfield.

6

It was a constant source of mortification to Jones that although he was surrounded by the supposed cream of today's youth, he found that he didn't understand them at all. In fact, he understood less and less about more and more. Huge changes that saddened and confused him were constantly taking place without his knowledge or consent and these changes, slyly effected, reached into every corner of human activity. Usually it was some time before he even noticed that they had happened. When did all the towns start to have exactly the same shops so that walking down a High Street, you couldn't tell which town you were in? When did football teams start having eight defenders instead of five forwards? When did people stop saying, 'It's up to him' and start saying 'It's down to him'? Who was there to monitor this linguistic U-turn? When did young people start to admire singers who couldn't sing? When did cars start to look alike so that you couldn't tell a Fiat from a

Ford? When did smokers suddenly become pariahs?

What the hell was going on?

His alienation was total, and as the class departed one afternoon at the close of a noisy seminar on idiom and dialect that had left the English language winded, wounded and, it seemed to Jones, terminally damaged, he stayed back at his desk, raking disconsolately through his papers and feeling that the will to live was more fragile than ever. The room smelt as if the world farting championships had recently been staged there and he went over to open some windows. Turning back into the room he saw that Rosemary Friedland, alone of the class, had stayed at her seat and was watching him closely. She still had the bow on the back of her head and he hoped that she would find it necessary to make some adjustments to it so that he could enjoy the startling profile of her chest.

'Can I help you, Rosemary?' he asked when he was back at his desk. It was almost unheard of for a student to hang about when the lessons were over.

'Who knows?' she said, putting papers into a folder. 'I've been worrying about my brilliant career.'

Jones was putting papers away himself. His plan now was to make his leisurely way to the Oasis of Sanity for a pain-free hour before he went home.

'What brilliant career is that?' he asked.

'I don't know,' said Rosemary Friedland. 'I haven't started it yet. Have you any idea what I should do?'

'One would hope that you would go on to university, giving you three years to learn a lot more, and three years to think about what you want to do with your life.'

Rosemary Friedland stood up. 'I had a wonderful brother and then he went to university and now he's a complete arsehole,' she said. 'He wants to be a tabloid journalist.'

'Well, there's money in it,' said Jones, looking at his watch. He wanted a cigarette but smoking was forbidden here.

'Waiting for a man called Nicholas to be convicted of stealing women's underwear so that you can head the story *"Knicker-nicker Nick is nicked"* seems a pretty forlorn way of earning a living to me.'

Jones looked up at this. It was when the seventeen-year-olds started to sound like twenty-seven-year-olds that his remorse at failing to understand them reached a peak. Perhaps his mistake was that he couldn't quite see them as adults although they increasingly sounded like them. Rosemary Friedland, with a shapely body tucked into a short summer frock, looked adult and, now he came to think about it, she talked and wrote like one.

'How old are you, Rosemary?' he asked. 'You sound about thirty.'

'Seventeen, Mr Jones, but I feel like thirty.'

Her papers safely tidied away, she walked across the room towards him now and, pausing only briefly, sat on the corner of his desk. 'You seem a sad man to me, Mr Jones. Do you wish you had some other job? As tabloid journalist, perhaps?'

'A bit late for that, Rosemary. But if I was setting out again I might well take a different path.'

'Exactly my point, Mr Jones. I could make a decision at my age that spoils my life. I don't suppose there's any chance of you buying me a drink?'

'I was under the impression,' Jones said nervously, 'that seventeen-year-olds weren't allowed to drink?'

'Oh, I almost never get taken for seventeen,' she said. 'You said yourself I sound like thirty and I look older than my age.'

Jones didn't care to dwell on those areas where she looked older than her age. The monstrous notion that she was actually trying to pick him up dawned slowly, and her knowing smile added to his uneasiness. It was not the first time that a flirtatious student had propositioned him, but it was the first time for many years. He had been younger and busier then and adept at brushing them off without causing hurt. Today, bereft of enjoyment, he felt strangely vulnerable.

'Anyway,' she said, 'if they make a big deal out of it I can always drink Pepsi.'

Jones felt the ground shifting beneath him and searched desperately for something to grasp. It would have been easier if the girl had stayed at her own desk but, sitting provocatively on his, her proximity distracted him and he found himself studying the shiny skin along the outside of one thigh. There were other things that he should have been looking at, but it was some time since he had even thought about girls' legs, let alone have them offered for his inspection at this close range.

'I suppose a Pepsi would be okay,' he heard himself mumble. 'We'll sort out your brilliant career.'

The deal done, she jumped off his desk and went to collect her folder while Jones stared vacantly at her receding bottom. He seemed to have moved from the tedious realities of the classroom to the stuff of dreams and as he stood and shuffled his papers he seriously wondered whether this *was* a dream, one of those wild escapist moments where sex still existed as a credible expectation that occasionally illuminated his sleep.

They drove in his old Vauxhall Nova, its grey paint stained by the thoughtless efforts of incontinent birds, to a public house in the country where cows, sheep and horses were their only witnesses. Rosemary Friedland blended into this environment as if she had already spent half her life in the public bar. When she asked for white wine the old lady behind the counter did not demur.

Jones drank whisky and felt his thoughts change. He looked at his student who was looking at him as if he presented a puzzle that she must solve.

'Have you ever thought,' she asked, 'of killing yourself?'

Jones reeled on his stool from the question. Was he that easy to read?

'Whatever makes you ask that?'

'You look the type. You look very nice, mind. Tall,

slim, nice face. But it's in the eyes. They're sad. There's a suicide every two hours in Britain. That's about four thousand a year.'

'The thought has occasionally drifted across my mind, I must admit,' he said. 'Life sometimes seems to be a series of pointless defeats.'

'It's ridiculous,' said Rosemary Friedland, licking the edge of her glass with a bright red tongue. 'You're a successful teacher.'

Jones laughed bitterly and turned away, instantly seeing himself in a mirror behind the counter. With his hangdog expression and his shabby clothes he didn't look like one of life's success stories. He looked like a man for whom the world was a continual and unrewarding struggle.

'Some things look like success and feel like failure,' he said. 'But we haven't come here to talk about me.'

'I figured you needed cheering up,' said Rosemary Friedland. 'I've been worrying about how sad you look.' She drank her wine, emptying the glass. 'I'm good at cheering people up.'

Jones looked in surprise at the empty glass. He had imagined that one glass of wine would be more than enough for a girl of seventeen.

'And how do you cheer people up?' he asked her.

'Oh, several ways,' she replied, shrugging. 'Some people like to play with my breasts.'

It took a moment or two for Jones to realise that his ears were not deceiving him, and several more for him to frame a reply. His own glass was empty now and he had no doubt that he needed another drink even if she didn't.

'Yes, I suppose that would cheer them up,' he said. 'I can see how that would brighten their day. Do you want another wine?'

She handed him the empty glass with a secret-ive smile.

'And then,' he said, 'we can get back to talking about you and your future.' She seemed to be rather closer to him than she had been when they sat down and his predominant emotion now was a jumpy nervousness. The conversation did not have the detached and academic flavour that he had intended, and he could easily see the pit of moral turpitude into which she could lure him with her body. But his determination to take the conversation one way was immediately baulked by her desire to lead it in a quite different direction.

'When most of the girls think about the future they don't think about their brilliant careers, they think about sex,' she said. 'In fact, most girls' ambitions don't go much beyond finding a man with a penis the size of an Italian waiter's pepperpot. I don't go along with that myself. I don't think size is important.'

Jones, temporarily deprived of the power of speech, waved the empty glasses at the old lady who, he was relieved to discover, was hard of hearing.

'Make mine a large one,' he said loudly, augmenting the message with a gesture with his hand. When he gave Rosemary Friedland her wine he found that she had switched the conversation again.

'You sometimes have the listless demeanour of a man who has given up,' she told him, with more than her usual assurance.

Jones took a hefty slug of whisky and tried to assert himself. 'Are we here to solve your problem or mine?' he asked. 'I thought you wanted to discuss the university option.'

Rosemary Friedland drank her wine as if it was Pepsi. 'Why not both?' she asked. 'You think you're imprisoned in a stereotype, but there's so much you could do. For a start I'd introduce some fun into your life so that it's not one long thankless drudge.'

'Oh?' said Jones, drinking more whisky. 'How would you do that?'

To answer, she took his hand and placed it on her breast. To have produced a similarly galvanic effect upon his body he would have had to plug two wet fingers into an electric socket. He pulled his hand away, shaking slightly.

'Christ!' he muttered. 'Don't do that.'

'We could walk in the meadows. We could talk to the animals and smell the flowers. We could fuck the arse off each other.'

'What?' The word caught in his throat and eventually emerged sounding like the voice of another man who has been hit brutally in the genitals at the moment of delivery.

'Why not?' said Rosemary Friedland, gaily ignoring

his discomfiture. 'To men a liaison with the opposite sex is a sort of extra-curricular activity that has no place in the mainstream of their lives.'

'I read that in an essay once,' Jones managed to say. He was trying to impose on himself the steely self-discipline that had carried him through twenty years of teaching without a single rebuke from those people who, mistakenly or not, sat above him in the educational hierarchy, but the whisky and the firmness of her breast conspired to weaken his resolve.

'I wrote it,' she said proudly, 'and I meant it. Nature intended a quick jump to propagate the species. It didn't expect us to build a lifetime's relationship on it.'

Impressed by this insight from one so young, he nevertheless managed to suggest, 'That isn't the way that young girls are meant to think. Public opinion is swinging against the one-parent family.'

'One parent's plenty, if you ask me,' she said. 'Nobody's trained for parenthood and few are any good at it.'

'I see,' said Jones. 'I see where you're coming from, as you young people say.'

'I can't admire my parents just because they're my parents. I'm a little more discriminating than that. Admiration has to be earned.'

'I see,' Jones repeated. There was a certain amount of role reversal going on here, and he tried to convince himself that if the student lectured the lecturer it showed what a good job the lecturer had done in the first place. Here was a young mind that was

83

working, evaluating and making mature judgements. It had been taught to think for itself and not accept the unremarkable opinions of others. He lit the cigarette that he had been waiting for and gazed into Rosemary Friedland's earnest face. 'It doesn't sound as if marriage is on your agenda.'

'I wouldn't like to be dependent on a man and I hope I never will be,' she said, finishing her second glass of wine with a boyish swig. 'Sex, yes. Subjugation, no.'

'I'm ashamed to admit I don't know what's happening to the younger generation.'

'We had some good teachers, Mr Jones, even if they don't have much confidence in themselves.'

'Who said they don't have any confidence in themselves?' The whisky was confusing him now and he wondered whether this was a reference to something that he had said and forgotten.

'Do you have the confidence for a walk in the meadow?'

He was on his feet before he had thought it through.

'Certainly I do. Let's go and look at the flowers.'

Early evening in the Oasis of Sanity, a tranquil languor that was quite different from the hustle and bustle that Colin Dunbar had envisaged when he bought the place hovered over the bar like a mist.

The only customer on his usual stool was Oscar Mansfield who today wore a maroon short-sleeve sport shirt that had attached to it a badge that said DON'T ASK. On the other side of the counter sat Colin Dunbar whose gaze flicked from his watch to the door as if at some pre-arranged moment his business would be swamped with customers. Both men had pints of lager.

'What's your official capacity in this establishment?' asked Oscar Mansfield.

'About ten pints a day,' said Colin Dunbar gloomily.

'I mean, are you the chef or the barman or the manager or what?'

'My wife cooks. I'm the cleaner, the cellarman, the business manager, the buyer, the washer-up, the chucker-out, the reservations clerk and the man who has to sit here and politely listen to people like you. Also, I'm the owner.'

'That's some job you've got there, Colin, baby. You should give yourself a rise.' Oscar Mansfield's untidy body shook with gentle laughter.

'Where *are* the customers, anyway?'

'I think they're eating Chinese this year.'

'Chinese?' said Colin Dunbar indignantly. 'What do they want to eat with bloody knitting needles for?'

The door opened and Julian Wyatt limped in wearing a damp grey tracksuit. His bouncy blond hair had been flattened by plumes of rain.

'You'll get fit, Julian, but the downside is you'll die of pneumonia,' Oscar Mansfield told him, laughing again. 'Alcohol or fruit juice?'

'Orange,' said Julian Wyatt, sitting on the first stool he reached.

'Have you had a good day?' Colin Dunbar asked him cheerfully. He had been told by somebody in the business that a bar was only as good as the customers it attracted, and he was concerned now that the maudlin trio who seemed to be his only regulars were not likely to encourage others to believe that dropping in here would improve the quality of their lives.

'A good day?' said Julian Wyatt incredulously. 'Let me run it past you. I began by cancelling a wonderful holiday I had planned for the family on the Tuscan-Umbrian border, and went on from there to a fraught lunch at Le Café des Amis in Hanover Square with a banker who did not succumb to my blandishments and extravagant hospitality in the way I had hoped. He even had the cheek to work in a lecture. A recession, says this humourless turd, is when money goes back to the people it belonged to. I resisted the temptation to put my fist through his brain, and went back to the office to discover that a little presentation on which we invested £6,000 has not won the account that we wanted, which has gone instead to a rather larger agency which could afford the gamble. Six grand down the drain. What sort of day have you had, Colin?'

'Bloody awful. I need Wyatt Promotions to bring me in some business.'

'It sounds like the blind leading the blind to me,' said Oscar Mansfield.

'What you want is a stunt that gets your name on the news pages. People don't seem to believe the ads any more.'

'LORD LUCAN SELLS SHERGAR TO ELVIS PRESLEY IN THE OASIS OF SANITY?' suggested Oscar Mansfield. 'Well within Julian's capabilities, I imagine.'

'I'll put my think tank on to it. Where's Jones? I always cheer myself up at this time of the day by seeing how miserable he is.'

'Perhaps he's topped himself,' said Colin Dunbar.

'Oh God, not yet,' said Oscar Mansfield. 'It's too soon for an insurance claim.'

In a field of corn exposed only to the curious gaze of swirling quail, Vernon Jones was fornicating like a goat on aphrodisiacs. Beneath him lay Rosemary Friedland, her eyes closed and her mouth open to allow for the gasps that repeatedly escaped during a sexual session that was lasting rather longer than she was used to.

'Boys come quicker,' she muttered at one stage, but Jones was not susceptible to conversation, particularly as he had a piece of corn up his nose and suspected, although he couldn't be sure, that not many yards away another couple were engaged in a similar pastime.

This was not what he'd intended when he set foot in the meadow, although the whisky allowed him to think that he had every chance of renewing his acquaintanceship with Rosemary Friedland's marvellous breasts. He hadn't begun to resolve the moral dilemma raised by this prospect when she removed her dress, bra and pants at a speed which made the whole operation look like the product of an animation artist at the Disney studios.

It had never occurred to him that among the pond-life that constituted his class there existed a generous creature like this. The nearest that most men got to a beautiful girl, he always told himself, was the television screen. He dropped the jacket that he was carrying over one shoulder as she started to undo the belt on his trousers. Her breasts jutted out untouched by gravity, like the air-brushed pictures in a sex magazine, and she flaunted them proudly.

'You don't want a broken-down old pedagogue like me, do you?' he asked as she pulled his trousers to the ground.

'Stick it in, Vernon, for God's sake,' she said. 'It's obviously in working order and we don't live for ever.'

The urgency and impatience of youth suddenly acquired a refreshing quality which made him feel outdated and staid. Anxious to join this action-loving fraternity, he pulled down his pale blue pants and relinquished what little control he had over the proceedings.

'You've got a nice body. It doesn't look a day over thirty,' said Rosemary Friedland, running a finger down his stomach. 'I see I please you.'

'Please please me more,' he said, pulling her towards him. Then she slid through his arms to the flattened corn that was to be their bed.

Now, as he pumped interminably towards a climax that showed no sign of arriving, he thought to stop and withdraw before he found himself facing the possibility of a pregnant student, but the sounds that were emanating beneath him suggested that this was not the moment to consider that.

'Christ!' said Rosemary Friedland eventually. 'That was the best ever. They say you need an older man.'

Jones, sprawled face down in the corn, hot, frightened and spent, found that his mind was working again with a clarity that it had lacked for much of the last hour.

'Blimey,' he said. 'What have we done?'

'A truly beautiful thing,' said Rosemary Friedland. 'I may write a poem.'

'Well, for God's sake don't bring it to the college. Look, I'd better drive you home.'

'No need,' she said, getting up. She looked down at him and smiled and then dressed almost as quickly as she had stripped. 'I only live half a mile from here and I'd better not arrive in your car.'

'Are you sure you're okay?' he asked, looking round for his clothes.

'I've never felt better.' She stepped out of the flattened area of corn where they had been lying and made a little waving gesture with her fingers. 'Cop you later, copulator.'

Jones sat up feeling dizzy and tried to find his pants. It was going to rain.

7

Nothing ever costs less than you expect, thought Julian Wyatt as he watched a man in overalls wrestling on his patio with equipment that had never been seen here before. The bills arrived with metronomic regularity and each was larger than he expected or hoped. Yesterday a routine service on the Range Rover had cost over £500. Today it was a blocked drain.

'It's no good poking round with a rod,' said the hired help. 'What it needs is a high-pressure jet.'

'And what will that cost?' Julian asked.

'Seventy pounds an hour, minimum two hours.'

'To clear a drain?'

'You want the job done properly, don't you?'

The final bill, including VAT, was £205 for a job that he had guessed would cost not much more than ten.

When the man had gone with his cheque, Julian Wyatt prowled around the garden and tried not to think about money. He had promised Lavinia that he would do some gardening this weekend, having been assured by the television weatherman that the rain would be torrential and unremitting. But as usual the sky was a clear blue and he was lumbered with duties that were more to Oscar Mansfield's tastes than his own. Soil needed turning, roses needed pruning, the lawn required iron liquid or whatever it was they used to keep grass a pleasant green rather than yellow or brown. There were other jobs here too, connected with the guttering, but his philosophy had always been that if you don't know how to do it you won't have to.

The self-punishment of jogging had produced aches in his calf muscles that made physical labour even less attractive than usual, and overcome by lethargy he slumped instead into one of the reclining chairs on the lawn. After all, it was his day off.

'The Englishman at work,' said his wife when she found him asleep in the chair twenty minutes later.

'I'm just gathering my strength,' he told her, surprised to have fallen asleep. It just shows, he thought, what the week's work is taking out of me.

'Well, I'm off to do the shopping,' said Lavinia. 'We've just been notified, by the way, that the school fees are going up.'

'Yes,' he said. 'I'm sure we have. What were these jobs you wanted done out here, if I manage to stand up?'

'When you've cut the grass and trimmed the hedge, could you tie those things back over there to the fence so they don't flop over the lawn? And could you dig that corner so that I can put in some new flowers from the garden centre?'

'Yes, my treasure.'

'I'm your treasure, and you're my treasurer. So don't forget about the school fees.'

When she had gone he found it difficult to stand up. The week's work would have exhausted him without the help of the jogging and the gym. But lying back in a peaceful vacuum with nothing to occupy his mind allowed the normal worries to trickle back. School fees! They were the last thing on your mind when you groped for a female thigh, but the world had a way of catching up on you.

Of more immediate concern was the monthly wages bill of £25,000. He found it almost impossible to believe that he was paying out that amount every month, but there were ten people in the office averaging £30,000 a year and that's what the monthly bill came to.

Almost the worst thing of all was the fact that he could no longer afford the little luxuries for himself, let alone the holiday he had just cancelled. He had always intended to buy a camcorder for the bedroom and he ruefully acknowledged a certain symmetry in the fact that he no longer had the money for it at the precise moment when his performances no longer justified the purchase.

Saturday was a sanctuary from the controlled mayhem of the college, but this morning Jones found that the enormity of his delinquency with Rosemary Friedland made it impossible for him to relax sufficiently to appreciate the break. His mind, spinning with a mixture of gratitude and guilt, had never left the cornfield. Wonderful sights were recalled, juicy moments relived and hideous consequences imagined. This latter aspect of his romp in the field crept up on him gradually; initially, he had been too proud and grateful to give it serious consideration. But now he began to wonder what unpleasant repercussions were in store. It was a gruesome possibility that Rosemary Friedland, that youthful nymphet, unhindered by abstract concepts like loyalty or discretion, would proudly discuss what she, in her innocence, would regard as a conquest; soon the whole college would know, and the dissemination of such gossip would not miss the radar ears of the Head. Jones's stance here would be outraged denial. It was hard to see how anything could be proved, and if it was his word against the girl's, the Head, on all known form, would lean towards him.

Pondering future problems as usual, he was interrupted by his wife.

'Are you coming to the shop?' she asked. A Saturday morning visit to the supermarket was a ritual they shared.

'Whenever you're ready,' he replied, and immediately heard a knock on the front door. He went out to open it, and discovered his doctor standing there with a folder under his arm.

'Good morning,' said Jones.

Beneath a mop of wiry grey hair, Dr Bradley had the smiling, boyish face of an actor from the jaunty world of satire; only a thick pair of horn-rimmed glasses conferred the gravity which the confidence of his patients demanded.

'Mr Jones, I'd like a word,' he said. 'May I come in?'

Jones, who had in the past experienced great difficulty in persuading a doctor to visit the house when he was actually needed, was so astonished to find one arrive without an invitation that he stepped back bemused and waved the doctor through. He followed him down the hall and directed him into the sitting room where the doctor looked at the stone fireplace and the cladding on the chimney breast as if he had never seen anything so tacky.

'It's like this,' he said when Jones had led him to the most comfortable armchair. 'How did the insurance thing go, by the way?'

'Signed and sealed,' said Jones. 'Thanks for the report.'

Dr Bradley nodded solemnly, a gesture which seemed to require his bottom lip to overlap his top.

'Well, it's like this,' he repeated. 'I was putting your papers away before surgery this morning and I happened to glance through them. I'm afraid I had a bit of a shock. The heart report wasn't as straightforward as I had thought. It turns out that you've had a mild cardiac infarction.'

'A what?' said Jones, alarmed.

'What we call a silent coronary. Ther's nothing to worry about. Well, hardly anything. You're symptom-free in every other respect, so you just soldier on. But what you've got to do, and what I've come round to tell you, is that you should take it very easily for a few weeks or we could have a major performance and find you on the floor. In a month or two we'll get you on to graduated exercises, but until then there should be no exertion at all. No cricket, no sex. Just rest.'

'No cricket?' said Jones.

'No sex,' repeated Dr Bradley.

Jones sat in the other less comfortable armchair and tried to absorb what he was being told. He had experienced no discomfort in his chest at all and yet here he was, apparently, teetering on the verge of death. The news petrified him.

'I can hardly believe it,' he said. 'I feel so well.'

'That's the cruelty of it, I'm afraid,' said Dr Bradley. 'But although you appear to be fit, you've had this infarction, and it's a warning we can't ignore. If we handle it properly, you'll be right as rain in no time, so don't start worrying because that won't help either.'

'Worrying is my natural condition, I'm afraid,' said Jones. 'What have I got to do?'

'A week's rest now is essential. You can take a gentle walk, it'll be good for you. Go to the shops, but don't carry heavy bags. Cut down on your smoking or, better still, cut it out. And the first thing is to take an aspirin every day. It reduces the chance of blood clots. I'll come to see you in a couple of days to see how you're getting on.'

'Blimey,' said Jones. 'This isn't good.' He felt more frightened than ever now and it made his heart beat faster which increased his fear.

Dr Bradley stood up. There were many calls to make. 'It's disconcerting, I know, but it's not that unusual. You're going to be fine as long as you obey these little rules I've set out. Cheer up, Mr Jones, and don't forget the aspirin.' He moved towards the door and saw that Jones was reluctant to get up. 'Don't worry,' he said. 'I'll let myself out.'

'What did he want?' asked Gaynor when she had heard the front door slam.

'He said I'm dying,' said Jones. 'Oh, he wrapped it up in medical terminology but that was the gist of it.' He sat in a daze, staring at the stone fireplace.

His wife sat down. 'What did he *actually* say?'

'A mild cardiac infarction. What he called a silent coronary.'

'A coronary?' said Gaynor. 'I've heard of that.'

'So have I,' said Jones. 'It kills people. It's what people of my age keel over from.'

'What did he say you must do?'

'Take it very easily. No work for a week — but it's half-term, anyway. Cut down on cigarettes. No exertion, no sex.'

'In other words, carry on as usual,' said Gaynor Jones with a secret smile. But she felt sorry for him when she saw the distress in his face.

'I'm the unexpected recipient of a death sentence,' he said, 'and I haven't made a will.'

Anger replaced fear as he began to realise the full significance of Dr Bradley's news. He felt a venomous misanthropy beside which his normal antipathy towards the human race bordered on affection. Why had the world singled him out for a visit from Dr Bradley this morning? Why couldn't he have dropped in on any of the other people who so eminently deserved this sort of blood-chilling message?

'A will?' said Gaynor Jones. 'You haven't got anything to leave, have you, apart from an old car and a cricket bat?'

'Oh, you'll be all right,' said Jones. 'The insurance will keep you in considerable comfort. Oh God,' he said, pausing, 'I'd forgotten Oscar's insurance. I suppose those three bastards will be off to the sun.'

This prospect intensified his misery and he struggled to his feet as if to prove that he wasn't finished yet.

'Let's go to the supermarket. The air will do me good,' he said.

'Would the doctor allow it?' Gaynor Jones's anxiety owed much to the fact that she would be deeply embarrassed if her husband collapsed in public.

'He said I can go to the shops but shouldn't carry heavy bags. You can trolley the stuff to the car.'

He put his hand to his heart as if a hand would help.

Susceptible though she was to the seductive attractions

and modish delights of the big department stores, Lavinia Wyatt's primary financial concern was for her temperamental twelve-year-old son Gavin and the school fees that would keep him in the exalted educational environment of Edgarley Hall in Somerset. If parents couldn't give their kids a good start in life, what use were they? And it wasn't only in Gavin's interest that he stayed at the school: his removal would be a social humiliation for Lavinia. To avoid this double disaster she was even prepared to generate some money herself if only she could work out how to do it. She had never been good at earning the stuff and, cushioned first by the generosity of her father and more recently by her husband, she had never needed to be.

These thoughts filled her mind as she drove the Range Rover into the free supermarket car park. It was crowded as usual and Daihatsu Sportraks jostled for parking spaces with Toyota Space Cruisers and Renault Espaces: the middle classes seemed to have abandoned conventional cars altogether. When she had effectively quenched the immediate parking prospects of two of them, she walked across to the supermarket and found Vernon Jones slumped on a wooden seat outside the store. He was wearing chinos and a tartan shirt and looked deathly pale. She was curious about his ashen appearance but had no intention of mentioning it. When you inquired politely about people's health they were always liable to tell you about it.

'Good morning, Vernon,' she said. 'Where's Gaynor?'

Jones pointed one thumb over his shoulder towards

the store. 'She's in there. Somewhere between the muesli and the Tampax, if I read her shopping list aright.'

Lavinia found Gaynor Jones between the muesli and the Tampax. She was studying a bottle of moisturising body lotion which had extracts of guava and kiwi.

'I'm glad I've bumped into you,' Gaynor said. 'I'd really appreciate a game of tennis some time.'

'That would be lovely,' said Lavinia Wyatt. 'It's so hard to find opponents during the week. Fay Dunbar's too busy and Emily's too old.'

Gaynor Jones dropped the body lotion into her trolley. 'Actually she's only a couple of years older than you.'

'Oh yes, we're the same age, but she's much older. What's the matter with Vernon? He looks pale.'

'He's had some bad news from the doctor. He's got a heart problem and needs to take things very easily. No exercise, no sex.'

'No sex?' said Lavinia Wyatt.

'The excitement would kill him. A lot of men have died having sex, he tells me. Attila the Hun and Nelson Rockefeller to name only two.'

'My God,' said Lavinia Wyatt. 'How's he taking it?'

'He's paranoiac. He thinks he's too frail for the hurly-burly of the supermarket. That's why he's sitting outside.'

'Poor Vernon.'

'Possibly,' said Gaynor Jones. 'On the other hand,

THE MYSTERY OF MEN

given the number of times he's discussed the attractions of suicide, you'd think he'd be more enthusiastic.'

'Oh Gaynor,' said Lavinia, mildly shocked. 'Are you sure sex would kill him?'

'So the doctor says. It's a strain on the heart at the best of times, as old Attila found. Not that Vernon's ever put too much strain on himself in that direction.'

'What are you going to do?'

'Play tennis. Keep fit. We can't have two invalids in the family, although I am probably going to end up in long-term therapy. That reminds me: I've got to get some aspirin. It reduces the chance of blood clots, apparently.'

'This is terrible news,' said Lavinia, hovering in the aisle. 'How old is he?'

'Forty-five, going on sixty. I don't believe it's as bad as he'd like to make out, frankly. They haven't rushed him into hospital, have they? Men are such hypochondriacs.'

'Sometimes it's too late for hospital,' said Lavinia Wyatt. 'They let them die at home.'

'Anyway, it will cheer up the boys with their little insurance plan. They'll see a pay-out coming up. How much do they get?'

'Thirty-three thousand each, isn't it? I'm sure none of them will be thinking about that.'

'Oh no?' snorted Gaynor Jones. 'I wouldn't put it past them. It's a disgusting scheme, and I can't think why they set it up. But then I've never understood men.'

Lavinia Wyatt looked at her with motherly concern. 'There's not a lot to understand, actually,' she said.

Outside Jones sat on his wooden seat, watching the world going about its business and wondered how many more times he would come here. If his life was nearly over it had certainly been a very quick affair. The years had shot by, and events that seemed recent to him, like Watergate and Ted Heath in Downing Street, were already embedded in the first half of his life. Years, arriving and disappearing at frightening speed, had shunted yesterday into the half-remembered past. His childhood sporting heroes were mostly dead. Old friends talked about their grandchildren instead of their children, and babies unborn when he started school were now in the Cabinet and ruling his life.

He considered the relative merits of cremation and interment.

8

In the Oasis of Sanity two days later there was an atmosphere of subdued expectation that induced feelings of shame and guilt in all those present.

'Credit me with foresight,' said Oscar Mansfield defensively, but the pervasive silence which greeted the news of Jones's misfortune did not allow anybody to credit Oscar with anything.

'I must admit,' said Julian Wyatt, 'that I always thought it was you who would end up on a life-support system.'

'I'm on a life-support system,' said Oscar. 'It's called a bar stool.'

'This isn't funny,' said Julian Wyatt reproachfully. 'Poor old Jones is a heartbeat away from eternity.'

'We all are, Julian,' Oscar said. 'It's something we have to live with. I myself occasionally feel a stabbing pain that reminds me I'm not here for ever.'

'Where do you get these stabbing pains?' asked Colin Dunbar.

Oscar Mansfield indicated his breastbone with the middle finger of his right hand. 'The sternum,' he said.

'That's practically fatal, kid,' said Colin Dunbar. 'I hope your bags are packed.'

Oscar Mansfield lit a cigarette and blew smoke thoughtfully at the oak beam above his head. An insouciant approach to such grave matters evidently struck the others as wildly inappropriate, but he had always believed that a solemn preoccupation with death was a ridiculous waste of what little time he had, given that death was something he could do nothing about.

'It doesn't seem right in here without the under-nourished image of Jones chatting enthusiastically about suicide,' he said. 'What's the news on him, any-way?'

'He's sitting at home taking things very easily,' Julian Wyatt told them. 'Lavinia dropped in to see him this afternoon.'

'She dropped in to see him?' said Oscar Mansfield, feeling pangs of resentment that pushed all sympathy for Jones into the background. 'She never drops in to see *me*.'

'You're not at death's door, Oscar. Lavinia was visiting the sick, like a good neighbour.'

Oscar Mansfield desired a visit from Lavinia Wyatt with a fervour he dared not admit to, and he wondered what ailments he could develop and promulgate to bring such a visit about. He imagined himself in bed wearing only a pyjama top, more or less stripped for action if

104

the opportunity for some sort of sexual entanglement presented itself.

'What I want to know,' said Colin Dunbar, 'is whether this sudden discovery of some heart malfunction would invalidate the insurance. It sounds as if there was a cock-up with his medical which the insurance people wouldn't be too happy about. Will they still accept it as kosher, or will they start arguing the toss?'

'In the event of Mr Jones's demise, do you mean?' asked Julian Wyatt. 'My God, you people can't wait to get your hands on the money.'

'Well, it's as well to know,' said Colin Dunbar, only slightly abashed. 'The Oasis of Sanity is in dire need of a cash transplant. What do you reckon, Oscar? You set the thing up.'

'The policies are in place. They can't wriggle now. If they did I'd go to the Ombudsman. You're looking at thirty-three grand all right, although, of course, we're all praying for Vernon's complete recovery.'

'Of course,' said Colin Dunbar, now appeased. 'I haven't got so many customers that I can afford for them to start dying.'

The bar was devoid of customers as usual but the door opened suddenly and a group of young people came in. They were of an age which might have worried another publican, conscious of the laws about under-age drinking, but, as he had just hinted, Colin Dunbar wasn't so lavishly endowed with clients that he could afford to start asking for birth certificates.

'What are you having?' he asked, expecting a shipping order for Coca-Cola.

In the event it was vodkas, spritzers and wines. One young man with a ponytail asked for a B.M.W. which Colin Dunbar had only previously heard of in connection with automobiles. It turned out to be Baileys, Malibu and whisky, which had the landlord despising the staid tastes of his regular customers. There were eight youngsters and the bill was more than £20.

'It would take you three visits to spend that much, Oscar,' said Colin Dunbar, visibly cheered by this infusion of money. 'Let these young people be an example to you.'

But Oscar, whose initial reaction was that of a man who suddenly discovers that a dozen gypsies have taken up residence in his front room, was now distracted by the conversation that he was overhearing. The group had withdrawn to a table in the corner of the bar but Oscar, whose hearing was famously acute and who boasted that he could hear himself blink, picked up all their words.

'I always wanted to come to this place but Jones is usually here,' said one.

'Well, he won't be in today. Rosemary's given him a heart attack.'

'What's she doing? Bonking her way round the staffroom?'

'She had Jonesy in a cornfield. She had Barratt in a van.'

'She had Nelson in the showers.'

106

Oscar listened to this in disbelief. His shock at the unseemly behaviour of a college lecturer was swiftly overridden by an insidious envy that Jones was having sexual relations with a girl of about seventeen — or, indeed, with anybody other than his rather surly wife. With one hand he brushed aside an offer of a drink from Julian Wyatt so that he could concentrate on the youthful conversation in the corner. It was obsessed, as he would have expected, with sex.

'I knew my sex-life was in ruins when I had a wet dream about Mrs Jarvis.'

'Mrs Jarvis the dinner lady? You *are* in a bad way, Mig.'

'Did you hear about Jason and Jackie? I'm not one to start a rumour, but they were exchanging chewing gum mouth to mouth this afternoon.'

The subject of Jones had evidently been exhausted and Oscar dropped his aural vigil and transferred his attention to the others.

'Now, Julian. What were you saying?' he asked.

'Nothing, Oscar. You weren't in the conversation.'

'Well, I'll just have the pint of lager I heard you offer, and thanks very much.'

'What was so interesting about the conversation you were eavesdropping? We know you can hear a mouse fart at two hundred yards.'

'The lager, Julian. The lager.'

The lager appeared and Julian Wyatt put coins on the counter.

'I wasn't eavesdropping, I was conducting an exploration into the complexity of adolescence,' said Oscar. 'However, I did hear something that you wouldn't believe.'

'Try me.'

'The invalid Jones has been knocking off a student. Sexual intercourse in a cornfield.'

'You're right. I don't believe you.'

'There's a girl at the college who, in their words, is bonking her way round the staffroom.'

'Even if there were, she would surely make an exception in Jones's case,' said Colin Dunbar.

'Apparently not. They all knew about it.'

Julian Wyatt looked across at the young people in the corner and wished that he was one of them. The world at that age was all jokes, sex and parties. But the idea that Jones had infiltrated their cheerful lives required an imaginative leap that was quite beyond him.

'Jones isn't a sexual person,' he said.

'He obviously has a secret side that we all missed,' suggested Oscar Mansfield.

'Pity he didn't miss it too, if he's got a dicky heart,' said Colin Dunbar. 'What's he trying to do — kill himself?'

'That's it,' said Oscar. 'The suicide expert has discovered the perfect suicide!'

That afternoon Lavinia Wyatt had sat naked in her bathroom exfoliating her armpits before applying a lotion composed of extracts of guava and kiwi to her freshly-washed body. She examined her long blonde hair and her statuesque figure in the full-length mirror and then, in a further orgy of purification, gargled with mouthwash and dabbed Chanel on her wrists before applying, in a fit of lustful extravagance, a mixture of unctions and colognes, essences and fragrances, to secret corners of her body.

It was a familiar routine. There was a man with money but superficial charm whom she met on a monthly basis for his health, and another younger man whose muscles had developed in the building trade, whom she met more frequently for hers.

But today's assignation was different, and as she drove the Range Rover towards Vernon Jones's rather drab bungalow she wondered whether she could produce in him the passion that she had come to expect on her other secret afternoons.

He greeted her with surprise, in an old blue shirt and grey trousers that he only wore when he was lounging around the house. From the sound that sprang from a room down the hall he had evidently been watching television.

'Gaynor's gone to London,' he said, visibly disturbed by this intrusion.

'Yes, I know,' she replied with a seductive smile. 'I've come to see you, to see how you are. You looked so worried outside the supermarket the other day.'

Jones was embarrassed. He had never encouraged visitors and didn't want them, but he could see that he could not leave her standing on the doorstep.

'Won't you come in?' he asked mechanically. 'Would you like a cup of tea? It's kind of you to call.'

She followed him into the sitting room, gliding down the hall with the confidence of a woman men desired, and perched on the arm of the sofa so that her skirt rode up her fleshy brown thighs.

'How are you feeling?' she asked.

'Very well, considering,' he said bravely, trying to play the host.

'You don't look too bad at all. You're a good-looking man, Vernon.'

Jones glanced uneasily at her big smile. How could she get all those teeth in her mouth and still have room for her tongue? The brown thighs reminded him of Rosemary Friedland sitting on his desk, and he could remember only too clearly where *that* had ended up.

'Gaynor thinks the doctor exaggerated,' he told her, for something to say. 'I don't think she believes him at all.'

'Naughty Gaynor,' said Lavinia Wyatt. 'How do you two get on, anyway?'

Jones laughed emptily. 'We're very happy together when we're apart.'

'That's sad,' said Lavinia, slowly undoing her dress. 'Why don't I make it up to you?'

Jones stopped dead, transfixed by what he was seeing. Her intentions were embarrassingly clear and, despite his aberration in the cornfield, this was not a situation in which he was comfortable.

'Oh, I don't know about that,' he said. 'I think perhaps I ought to make tea.'

'Tea?' said Lavinia Wyatt. 'No thanks.' Her dress slipped to the floor and she was wearing some pink diaphanous garment and no pants. 'Come on, Vernon. I've come to console you.'

His mind went blank. 'What about Gaynor?'

'Gaynor's at the V and A.'

'But we don't know,' he said nervously, 'what time she'll get back.'

'Yes, we do,' said Lavinia. 'She'll get back at six.' She was an expert at covering her tracks and had already decided, because the neighbours had seen her arrive here, that she would tell Julian that she had paid a social call on Jones. It would sound so innocent that he would commend her humanitarian instincts. 'Your hang-ups are becoming an obstacle to my pleasure, Vernon. Didn't they teach you not to keep a lady waiting?'

She stood up. It was obviously going to take total nudity to nudge this lummox into action. She shrugged her shoulders and the diaphanous underwear fell to her feet.

'What do you think of me?' she asked, hands on hips.

Jones stared at the physical attributes that were paraded before him in stark incomprehension. For years the solitary peak of his erotic experiences had been a glance at the pictures of topless secretaries that appeared in the downmarket newspapers abandoned by colleagues

111

in the college staffroom, but now, twice in one week, attractive and desirable females had, without a hint of encouragement from him, whipped off their clothes and defied him to ravage their lovely bodies. There was something almost Biblical about the incongruity of it, as if Other Hands had taken matters over and decided that the time had arrived for Jones to be tempted and tested, before being offered a superior position in another world.

But Jones, aroused now, had no hopes or beliefs of another world and after the setbacks he had experienced lately he knew that the correct reaction to temptation was to succumb. He yanked off his trousers with a balletic grace that owed something to his rehearsal in the cornfield, and was relieved to see that his ailing, infirm body, consigned to the junk heap by enlightened medical opinion, was attached quite firmly to an erection like a police baton. For a moment he felt young again. If, during his long years of non-participation, women had become the predator and not the prey, it was a quantum leap forward so far as he was concerned.

'The sofa,' said Lavinia Wyatt, 'like this.' She lay back on the cushions with her legs apart and held out her arms. What I've got here, she thought, is a sex maniac with a weak heart.

Jones was on his knees almost immediately, kissing her legs and thighs.

'Do you recognise the body lotion?' she asked. 'Your wife uses it, doesn't she?'

'I've never smelt it before,' said Jones, trying to extract a pubic hair from between his teeth.

With a strength that surprised him she pulled him up to her, so that his face was buried in her neck. He had forgotten that she was rather a good tennis player and had shoulders of hidden power.

'This will do you good, Vernon,' she murmured, worried now that he might expire before he had begun. 'I'm sure you can remember how to do it.'

'You're a sorceress, Lavinia,' he told her. 'In your arms all things are possible.'

It was Oscar Mansfield, he thought, who had always given the impression that he fancied Lavinia Wyatt. Jones, when he noticed her at all, thought her tarty and rather dim. But confronted by this cornucopia of flesh, such negative thoughts seemed hypercritical and they quickly dissolved in the heady fusion of aromas that now overpowered him. Lavinia Wyatt lay back with her eyes closed and a slight smile on her lips, while Jones seemed to be bent on unscrewing her left breast.

'You need me, don't you, Vernon?' she said.

'Knead you?' said Jones, absently licking a nipple.

'My body is yours.'

Responding to this imperative, Jones relinquished the breast and entered her with a vigour that took her by surprise. She had imagined that she would be nursing an invalid through the physical demands of lovemaking, but the boisterous passion which Jones now evinced made her contemplate the unforeseen possibility that she might have an orgasm herself. She nearly did, but was distracted by the objective of her mission. She lay there afterwards with Jones sprawled on top of her showing every sign of having fallen asleep.

'Vernon,' she said.

'Mmmm?' said Jones.

'Time to get up.'

'Mmmm,' said Jones.

'Gaynor's due home.'

Jones opened his eyes and eased himself off her. Lavinia Wyatt looked at him, expecting a seizure or a convulsion, but he appeared to be rather well.

'How do you feel now?' she asked.

'Marvellous,' he said, starting to put on his clothes. 'You were right. It *is* good for you.'

She stood up, puzzled, and began to get dressed herself. Perhaps the harmful effects of his exertions would take some time to show. Perhaps he would be found collapsed after she had left. Perhaps she ought to do it again as soon as possible, imposing a cumulative strain on his vulnerable heart.

'Would you like to do it again some time?' she asked. 'I enjoyed that.'

'I certainly would,' said Jones. 'I don't have afternoons like that very often.'

'How about Thursday? I believe Gaynor is at the tennis club.' She looked at her watch. 'I've got to go.'

He escorted her to the door.

'Thursday would be fine,' he told her.

'*Hasta mañana*, Vernon.'

'No, Thursday,' said Jones.

It was only when she had swept away in her Range Rover with a girlish wave, and the excitement and tumult of the last hour had been replaced by a peaceful calm which enabled him to think, that he remembered with a shock that he was not supposed to submit himself to the rigours of sex. Of course, he thought bitterly, when he *was* supposed to, there wasn't any to submit himself to. But the thought frightened him and he decided to cancel Thursday. At the same time he couldn't deny that he felt a lot better than he had this morning and he wondered whether perhaps there were beneficial effects to be had from the afternoon's activities. He even wondered fatalistically whether there was much sense in passing up the opportunity to enjoy Lavinia Wyatt's lovely body if he had such a limited lifespan.

But later, when he was relaxing in the luxury of a warm bath, his head had cleared sufficiently for him to fall upon another even less pleasant possibility which his brain, clouded by lust, had completely missed: Lavinia had been trying to kill him for the insurance money.

9

Hurtling west in the Range Rover at a little over ninety miles an hour, Julian Wyatt counted the cost of a day away from the office and miserably enumerated the things that could go wrong in his absence. Beside him in the front passenger seat his wife was studying a magazine article about the New Bourgeoisie that was designed to tell whether or not she was middle class. It was a designation she greatly coveted.

'"Every detail of your lifestyle holds a clue to your social status",' she quoted. 'Do you think we're middle class, darling?'

Julian Wyatt swerved dexterously into the outer lane to overhaul a blue Volvo. 'I don't,' he said slowly, 'give a monkey's fuck whether we are or not.'

'Oh dear,' said Lavinia Wyatt. 'Driving makes you so tense.'

'It's life that makes me tense,' he answered.

The previous day when he had foolishly taken the

Range Rover into London, a white youth who was unusually fleet of foot had shattered his side window with a hammer, stolen his portable phone from the driver's seat, and sprinted away in the crowd. Plenty of people had watched him — that's how he knew the boy was white — but none had the energy or inclination to impede his escape. The new window had cost more than £500. Little things like that, on top of his other burdens, sometimes threatened to tip him over the edge.

'We qualify on the grounds of job, salary and house, but we're a bit dodgy on hobbies and leisure,' said Lavinia.

'Oh? What are we supposed to do with our leisure?'

'Ski, ride horses, play golf, collect antiques. We should belong to clubs and societies apparently.' She continued studying the magazine when he failed to respond. 'We're not too good on holidays, either, now we can't afford them. It's got to be a villa in Tuscany or walking in the Pyrenées. Shopping trips to New York are okay, too.'

'Oh good,' said Julian Wyatt. 'We must save up.'

'Drinks on the sideboard. Armagnac, champagne, Laphroaig malt whisky, vintage port.'

'We've got some of those. Couldn't we be semi-middle class?'

'Children's names. We've really blown it here. Oliver, Thomas, Alexander, James, Daniel, Matthew and Joshua.'

'Pity you called him Gavin really. It's your working-class roots showing through.' The possibility of a smile lingered briefly over his stress-filled face.

'I'm not ashamed of my working-class roots,' she protested.

'Well, stop trying to penetrate the bourgeoisie then,' he said irritably.

'Here's where we score,' she said, refusing to be diverted. 'First-time buyers of private education for the children.'

'I wonder how the little sod is?'

Their mission today was to collect their son for his ten-day half-term holiday, and as they cruised over the round hills of Somerset they wondered what beneficial effects he was getting from his expensive education. At the age of twelve, Gavin Wyatt had his father's blond hair, his mother's calculating gaze, and a sullen irreverence that was all his own.

Edgarley Hall, junior school for the more famous Millfield, was sprawled over ninety acres on the slopes of Glastonbury Tor. Apart from the things that would normally be found in a school, it had an indoor swimming pool, a nine-hole golf course, a music school with a recital hall, a shooting range, five science laboratories, a language development centre, separate pitches for football, rugby, hockey and cricket, and numerous courts for netball, tennis and squash. When Julian Wyatt thought back to the grimy portals of his secondary school, he could only wonder what these magnificent facilities were going to produce.

Gavin stood waiting with his suitcase at the pick-up point in front of the low, greystone buildings. He had grown two inches.

'Hi,' he said, one hand raised in greeting.

'Hallo darling,' said Lavinia Wyatt, dispensing with the trendy formalities and kissing him on the cheek. 'My, you're tall.'

'How are you, Gav?' asked Julian Wyatt, shaking his hand. 'Ready for a rest from all this work?'

'It's been very enjoyable, actually,' said Gavin, climbing into the Range Rover. 'I've taken up judo, karate and fencing.'

'Blimey,' said Julian Wyatt. 'About all I took up at school was conkers.'

They headed south past green fields to pick up an east-west trunk road.

'You can see why they call it a green and pleasant land,' Lavinia Wyatt remarked. 'It's difficult sometimes to remember how beautiful it is.'

This mild observation, which she had imagined might extract polite murmurs of assent from either or both of them, provoked instead a dissonant note from the rear of the vehicle which took them both by surprise.

'Don't give us all that "British is best" baloney again, Mum. I'm too old to believe it any more.'

Lavinia Wyatt glanced at her son over one shoulder. 'What baloney is that, darling?'

'Oh, you know. British justice is the best in the world. That was a good one. Do you know how many people have been released from prison lately after serving years for murders they never committed? Twenty? Thirty? The British bobby is the best in the world — that was another one. It's the police who fitted the poor men up, concealing evidence and making up confessions.'

'Yes, well,' said Lavinia, looking at her husband for some support.

'Anything else?' asked Julian Wyatt. 'I see they've got your brain in gear.'

'Yes, politicians,' said Gavin, leaning forward in his seat. 'You told me when I was a kid that they were the most honourable in the world. Devoting themselves to the service of the country was what you told me, Mum. What a load of old horse manure that's turned out to be. If they're not poking sleazy tarts in borrowed flats, they're taking a lot of money in brown envelopes to ask questions in Parliament, and God alone knows what else. Bung them the moolah and they'll do *anything*.'

Obliged though he felt to acknowledge the truth of this, Julian Wyatt fell silent. The little speech had depressed him. It was only partly because his son failed to share his enthusiasm for Britain, its noble traditions and celebrated freedoms. More ominously, there was the nagging feeling that he had been left behind, clinging to outdated ideas, and a new generation had arrived who saw things he didn't and refused to share his beliefs and didn't want to share his company or his country.

'What was it Dad used to say?' asked the disputatious voice behind him. 'Britain is the workshop of the world. Have you looked in a car park lately? Do you know *anybody* who has a television made in Britain?'

'I think I said that it *used* to be the workshop of the world.'

'Yeah, about a hundred and fifty years ago. This country's wrecked. As soon as I'm old enough I'm off to Australia, the America of the next century.'

'I don't think so, Gavin,' said Julian Wyatt, relieved to find something that he could refute. 'They've sold the family silver. Iron-ore rights to Japan and all that.'

But the prospect of her only child putting half a world and 12,000 miles between them had a curious effect on Lavinia Wyatt. She started to cry.

'Don't say that, darling,' she said, wiping her eyes. 'I want you here.'

'In this green and pleasant land, Mum? Have you taken a walk on your own after dark lately? Women get raped today by men who have stopped to *help* them.'

'I think you're upsetting your mother,' said Julian Wyatt. He had reached the main road now and he put his foot down, more out of frustration than a desire for speed.

'I'm sorry, Mum,' said Gavin, 'but we can't be parochial any more. We're citizens of planet Earth.'

'I'm sure we can stop being parochial without emigrating to the other side of the world,' said Lavinia Wyatt. 'We have a nice country.'

But this bromide was too tiresome for him to consider. 'We even cocked up the Channel Tunnel,' he said, after a little pause. 'It should have been a road so that we can drive straight into Europe. Europe's got nothing to learn from us, but we've got a hell of a lot to learn from Europe.'

'One school trip to France has evidently broadened your mind,' said Julian Wyatt.

'We went to Switzerland, too,' said his son. 'And, yes, it did open my eyes. You walk around Geneva and you know straight away that you're not in Britain.'

'I suppose the traffic being on the right-hand side is a bit of a giveaway?'

'That and the trains,' said Gavin Wyatt, 'which are spotless and punctual to the second. In Britain the trains are filthy, late and apt to break down. Why do you think that is, Dad?'

But Julian Wyatt had had enough of this conversation now and was beginning to count the days until the end of half-term. He had problems aplenty to solve at Wyatt Promotions, without trying to untangle the manifold and no doubt intractable ones that beset the apparently disintegrating entity they called Great Britain.

His mind roamed over the lengthening list of predicaments and pitfalls that confronted him. His working life seemed to be an endless quest to make ends meet that remained many miles apart. But then, as he drove along on a sort of automatic pilot and his wife succeeded in engaging their son in a conversation that steered clear of conflict and strife and concentrated peacefully on the mundane events at school, he had an idea that lifted his depression.

Sell the house! It would release capital and give him time to breathe. Later, when the business was flying, he would buy another one.

He could instantly see the estate agent's brochure: '*A detached period house with part-walled garden, said to date from the early nineteenth century and subsequently considerably extended.*' He would slap the place on the market for £300,000 and stop kowtowing to the banks. Of course, with his debts the banks had a charge on the house but there would be money to spare when that debt was settled. He would rent a little place for a year while he regrouped and revitalised his forces. Their house was too big anyway.

The move would dismay his wife, but a dose of reality was what she needed. Better still, it would be a salutary jolt for the confident little bastard in the back seat. No gratitude ever emanated from his vituperative son. Gavin showed no signs of appreciating the effort he was making, or understanding the stress that he was enduring. Food, clothes and money were accepted with casual ingratitude as if they had been plucked from the trees. There was no indication that he was aware of the sacrifices that lay behind his education, and he planned to repay the debt by disappearing at the first opportunity to Wagga Wagga or Wollongong, so desperate was he to enjoy his parents' company once he had shaken off the shackles of school.

Billet the little sod in a tent, he thought, and see how that grabs him. Cut his pocket money, sell his records, halve his meals, cart his precious wardrobe to the Oxfam shop.

He glanced at his son's brooding face in the rearview mirror and started to whistle.

Dear Sir, wrote Emily Mansfield on one of her large sheets of blue paper. *Your columnist blithely asserts that the Royal family cost me no more than the equivalent of a packet of cigarettes a week. But the Queen is the richest woman in Britain, and I am one of the poorest. Wouldn't any rational person concede that it would be more equitable if she subsidised me?*

Satisfying though the letter was, she still had bile to discharge, and her Parker pen hovered over the next sheet while her mind searched for targets.

Dear Sir, she wrote. *Given the Pope's animosity towards women and his hostility towards contraception, shouldn't the Roman Catholic Church be a men-only organisation, rather like the Masons, with the occasional Ladies' Night to appease the lesser sex? The men would be able to concentrate on gleaning advice about their love lives from celibate geriatrics, while the wives enjoyed the company of condom-carrying heathens.*

There was another little fusillade waiting in the barrel but as she struggled to remember it she was interrupted by the appearance of Adrian, her fourteen-year-old son, who was obviously in his usual ferment of apathy. He fell into an armchair and announced: 'I'm bored.'

Emily's faith in the reliability of geneticists, or any other group of specialists whose faculty leaned towards the hard ground of science rather than the airy-fairy machinations of the mind, faltered when she studied her son. The virtues which she told herself she possessed, like energy, enthusiasm, an inquisitive mind and a questioning nature, had not even reached her only son in diluted form. She had, of course, to consider the unfortunate contribution made by the sex-change transvestite who sired him, and it was this element, the responsibility for which she could hardly avoid, that caused her to bring more sympathy and understanding to her relationship with Adrian than he probably deserved.

'Bored, darling?' she said. 'Why don't you read a book?'

'Books are boring, Mum,' said Adrian, and she tried to remember when she had last seen him pick one up. 'What's on television?'

'Nothing worth occupying your mind,' she said.

He was a pale youth with fair hair, and sometimes in photographs he looked as if he was fading away, like the face on the Turin Shroud. Emily Mansfield worried about him with a helpless zeal. She had often thought that it would take the intensive care of private education to bring him out of himself, as the Wyatts had done with their boy, but she was reluctant to lay the burden of school fees on her second husband who, she often felt, had taken on quite enough with her.

'It's your half-term, Adrian,' she said. 'It's summer. Why don't you go camping, or cycle to the coast or play cricket or go fishing or swimming or something?'

'Too boring,' said Adrian.

'Only boring people are bored, young man,' she said. 'Unless of course they're pinned to the wall at a party by someone they can't get rid of.'

Oscar Mansfield came in from the garden where he had been pruning his roses and soaking the lawn with soluble lawn food.

'How are you, Adrian, you little hive of activity?' he asked.

'He's bored,' said Emily. 'Or so he keeps telling me.'

Oscar was wearing a little beret that made him look like a French onion-seller, and a red T-shirt which bore the message: *If only Eve had taken the Pill*. He sat down and studied his dirty hands. The challenge of arousing some interest in his sluggish stepson was one that he had faced many times before and he seldom met with much success. Today he had a new idea.

'I'll pay you ten pounds,' he said, but couldn't think what the boy could do to merit the money.

'Yes?' said Adrian, displaying a glimmer of interest. Oscar could see that, as with many people much older than Adrian, it was only the certain prospect of banknotes that would produce the energy necessary to get him off his backside. He thought immediately of

127

the garden, but such help as the boy had ever offered there had produced effects contrary to those he had wanted: not only did he have to do the job himself again afterwards, but the job itself was somehow larger by that time than it had been before Adrian started.

'Give him something creative to do,' said Emily. 'Get his brain working. Menial jobs don't seem to suit him.'

'What do you suggest?'

'Paint a picture. Paint a picture of the house from the back garden. You're great at art, Adrian.'

'I don't think so,' said Oscar Mansfield. He could see the boy knocking out a picture in no time and demanding the money. He'd be back within the hour telling them that he was bored. Glancing at the table where his wife had evidently been writing a few angry letters, he had a better idea.

'Get yourself a notebook and write me an account of a day in your life, starting from now.'

'What a good idea,' said Emily. 'You can write about what you do and see and think.'

'And it will take a whole day,' said Oscar.

'For ten pounds?' said Adrian.

'That's the deal. You can sit in the garden or go out on your bike or do whatever you want, but I've got to have at least five hundred words. Okay?'

Adrian nodded, stood up and slouched from the room

'That was a good idea, darling,' said Emily Mansfield. 'Are there any more where that came from?'

'Yes,' said Oscar. 'I'm taking you both out to dinner at the Oasis of Sanity tomorrow night. It's my birthday, in case you've forgotten.'

'Sell the house?' said Lavinia Wyatt. 'Are you going mad?'

'No, I'm going broke,' her husband replied, 'and yet we've got all this money locked in bricks and mortar.'

'And where are you suggesting we live? In a portable cabin?'

'We'll rent a house, my dear. In Germany, that bastion of middle-class prosperity, they do little else.'

Lavinia Wyatt was cutting up runner beans in the kitchen, beans they had stopped to pick at a country market on the way home from Somerset. She wanted to provide a special dinner on his first evening home for her son who was upstairs unpacking, but her enthusiasm for the occasion was wilting under the weight of bad news. First Gavin wanted to emigrate, now Julian wanted to sell the house. She felt as if fate was mechanically chipping away at the foundations of her life.

'I like this house,' she said. 'It suits us.'

'Wise up,' said Julian Wyatt, plunging a corkscrew into a bottle of Valpolicella. 'If the banks pull the plug on Wyatt Promotions we'll lose the house anyway and not get a penny. This way we'll get cash and time.'

'And then everything will be all right, will it?' she asked. The forecasts had been so pessimistic for so long that she now felt that only her own efforts would produce the money they needed.

'Who knows?' said her husband, extricating the cork. 'All I know is that in this financial climate you can only soldier on and keep your fingers crossed. We sure as hell would never sell the firm.'

Lavinia Wyatt lifted the beans into a large saucepan of boiling water.

'It always comes down to money in the end, doesn't it?' she said.

She took her joint of roast beef from the oven and wondered how Vernon Jones was feeling.

IO

The prospect of expiring between the silken thighs of Lavinia Wyatt had lost what small allure it had ever possessed by the time that Jones got out of bed on Thursday morning. He had developed a sick man's determination to fight, combined paradoxically with a perfectly fit man's understandable reluctance to be prematurely dispatched to the hereafter with a post-humous hard-on. He decided to ring her and cancel.

The call had to wait until Gaynor had left for the tennis courts, and when he rang the Wyatts' home there was no reply. He waited a while in case she had been in the garden or the bathroom, and then rang again but no one answered. The seductress, he imagined, was already in transit.

He went into the sitting room, sat down in the best armchair and wondered how best to convey to Mrs Wyatt that he was not available for the sexual spectacular that she anticipated. Given that the bitch was trying to kill him, he considered how marvellously offensive he could be. Should he tell her that he had guessed her intentions and if it was money she was after, she had better get out on the street and earn it? Should he mention his disappointment when he realised that she was trying to finish him off?

He got up and headed for the kitchen to make himself a coffee and was greeted by the strident call of the telephone in there. Jones had always hated telephones and found insulting their implicit assumption that he had nothing better to do with his time than get up and respond to an unknown caller, a grievance which he seldom bothered to disguise as he jammed the receiver into his neck. He glared at the machine and told himself that a ringing telephone was an invitation, not a command.

But then it occurred to him that the caller was probably Lavinia Wyatt and he could save her wasting time on her ruthless and degrading mission, and himself a lot of nervous tension. He picked up the phone.

The caller was Dr Bradley who said: 'Mr Jones? Thank God I've caught you in!'

'Oh, hallo,' said Jones, confused by the identity of the voice.

'I'm sorry about this, Mr Jones. I'm really sorry.'

My God, thought Jones, sitting down. This is the voice of the death sentence, deep, emotional and littered with 'sorries'.

'I really owe you a huge apology and don't quite know what to say,' said Dr Bradley in the emollient tones that he used at bedsides. 'I've just had Vincent

Jones in here to see me and you could guess what I've discovered, couldn't you? His papers were put in with yours. I'm afraid that to a receptionist, one V. Jones is very like another. It's he who had the mild cardiac infarction, not you. You're as sound as a bell.'

'What?' said Jones.

'I can't tell you how sorry I am, but these things do happen in the best regulated circles and nobody could accuse my surgery of being that. The other Mr Jones had an electro-cardiogram and we thought the report had been mislaid. We searched everywhere and then found it in your folder.'

'What?' repeated Jones.

'It's a shock, I can tell. But the good news is, Mr Jones, that your heart is A.I.'

'Well, thank you, Doctor Bradley,' said Jones. 'It is a bit of a shock — you're right.'

'You can stop taking the aspirins and get on with your life.'

'My life?' said Jones, feeling terribly vague.

'Yes,' said Dr Bradley. 'Put this unfortunate mistake from your mind and enjoy yourself.'

Jones replaced the receiver but did not get up. His capacity for absorbing startling news and sensational occurrences had grown rapidly in the recent past, but Dr Bradley's revelation produced a mood of exhilaration that was quite alien to his normal melancholy disposition. He was about to jump up and do a little dance, confident that the exercise would no longer damage his health, when there was a knock at the front door. He was so preoccupied with the change in his fortunes that he wondered who it could be.

Lavinia Wyatt posed voluptuously on the doorstep in the sort of mini-skirt he hadn't seen for years.

'Lavinia!' he said. 'Come in!'

'Have you got something for me?' she asked coyly, stepping over the threshold.

'I've been saving it for you,' he said, feeling the stirrings of desire.

'How are you feeling?' she asked, sitting down on the sofa where they had performed so energetically before.

'Not too bad,' he said. 'Surprising really.'

She patted the cushion beside her. 'Sit here,' she said.

Jones responded to this innocuous proposition by removing his trousers. 'Let's get on with the business, Mrs Wyatt, and not waste time on chat. We're talking tumescence here.'

Lavinia Wyatt, her mind on quietus rather than coitus, realised that she must respond to this strange behaviour without delay. She slid down a pair of pink briefs and kicked off her stiletto shoes. The mini-skirt rode up round her waist. Jones fell on her like a drowning man within reach of a liferaft.

They made love on the sofa as they had before and ten minutes later did it again, rather more slowly, on the white shag carpet. Finally, in a mood of elation created by the news from Dr Bradley, he gave her another one against the door, bruising her buttocks on the handle; but it was an experience

Lavinia Wyatt appeared to welcome, judging by her encouraging noises.

When Jones had finished and wandered off to find his trousers she studied him closely, irritated that he was still vertical and mobile. If anything, he looked younger and fitter than when she arrived.

'You're astonishingly virile, Vernon,' she said, aggrieved.

'Aren't I?' he said. 'Do you want coffee?'

'I can't stay. I'm supposed to be playing tennis, too.'

Ten minutes later she staggered from the bungalow, sore and disorientated, wondering how a powerful man like Attila, the King of the Huns, could defeat the Roman Emperor but die making love, while an invalid like Jones could fornicate repeatedly like a prize bull and then offer her coffee.

The arrival of his forty-first birthday was not, so far as Oscar Mansfield was concerned, cause for celebration, but his wife expected such occasions to be marked by something or other, and she had promised the Dunbars at the barbecue that they would eat soon at the Oasis of Sanity and provide them with that rare commodity, paying customers.

With Adrian in tow, they took a table in the corner and examined a menu of surprising variety: lasagne with langoustines, artichoke with truffles. There was a dessert of wild strawberries in lime parfait. Emily Mansfield was baffled by the public's changing tastes and fads — in food and clothes as much as in television, films and music — and felt increasingly divorced from them. She ordered lamb, Oscar had salad and fish, and Adrian chicken.

'And a wine with lots to say for itself,' Oscar told Colin Dunbar as he took the order. 'My love to the chef.'

Having received a silk tie for his birthday, Oscar felt obliged to wear it and no longer resembled the somewhat untidy man who lolled at the bar counter every evening. Emily, who dressed for comfort and not for men, wore an old green two-piece.

'So,' he said to Adrian who had today shaken off the persistent vegetative state which seemed to be his normal condition, 'how is my essay coming along?'

'It's finished,' said Adrian. 'I've done it.'

'It's finished? Where is it?' asked Emily.

'It's at home. I didn't think you'd want to read it over dinner.'

'I look forward to it,' said Oscar. 'Is it good?'

'I think so,' said Adrian. 'I think it will surprise you. Can I have an orange juice, please?'

Oscar turned to call to Colin Dunbar and saw Jones come through the door. Dire presentiments of an untimely end seemed, if anything, to have made him look more cheerful.

'I didn't know you were a *bon vivant*, Oscar,' he called.

Jones could not remember when he had felt better. The worries that had beset him even before he had been told he had a heart condition had receded with the good news about his health. Thoughts of suicide had suddenly become a distant memory: there was a time to live and a time to blow your head off, but suicide would be a curious option when beautiful women kept throwing their naked bodies at you.

He considered the two women and wondered whether, now that he was becoming familiar with the energetic charms of Lavinia Wyatt, it wasn't time for a return to the cornfield to enjoy again the youthful appreciation of Rosemary Friedland. It seemed incredible to him that with his age and status, he actually had a choice and could take his pick from two females that most men would pay money to get their hands on. He obviously possessed hidden charms that he, in his self-effacing and defeatist way, had never imagined were his.

Once half-term was over he would pay some attention to Rosemary Friedland and see what invitations she dangled before him. If nothing developed he would offer her extra coaching and the guarantee of success in her exams; it was not something that a student would turn down, but it was something that could lead to other things, notably a Rosemary Friedland without any clothes on — a prospect which stirred him instantly despite his exhausting morning with Mrs Wyatt.

He walked up to the counter and asked Colin Dunbar for a lager.

'How are you, Vernon?' he asked. 'We've been worried about you.'

'Well, worry no longer,' said Jones. 'It was all a mistake. The doctor had the wrong V. Jones. Marvellous, isn't it?'

'That's terrific,' said Colin Dunbar miserably. 'That's really wonderful news.'

'I knew you'd be pleased,' said Jones. 'Pity about the Caribbean cruise, though.'

'I suppose that would account for the wild oats in the cornfield?' asked Colin Dunbar, not pleased at the thought of what he had missed.

'The what?' said Jones, putting down his drink.

'I read it in the paper. Randy teacher in leg-over shock.'

'Don't jest with me, Colin,' said Jones, with a rapt attention that he had often hoped to inspire in his students. 'What are you telling me?'

'Oh, there were some kids in here. Your name was mentioned in connection with a girl in a field.'

'Get me another drink,' said Jones, emptying his glass.

But by the time he had produced it, Colin had to revert to his other role of waiter. There was food to be delivered to the Mansfields' table and other diners had now come in and were studying the menu. Good food, if not the jaundiced company at the bar, was pulling in business tonight.

Jones sipped his lager and juggled possibilities. Kids boasted and gossiped, not believing what they were hearing half the time. But there was something daunting about the mention of a field — it was too specific for comfort. He could hardly wait for Colin to return from his alternative duties.

'What did the kids say?' he asked.

'I don't know. It was Oscar who was listening to them. One of your female students has a bit of a reputation, I gathered.'

Jones found this uniquely deflating, and temporarily lost sight of the wider threat raised by his reckless behaviour becoming common knowledge. If Rosemary Friedland shared her favours with whoever was in the queue, it took the shine off his own little romp. Mentally, he withdrew his offer of extra tuition and tried instead to imagine which way the bad news would spread.

'What was she like?' asked Colin. 'I haven't had a seventeen-year-old since, oh, since I was seventeen.'

'Don't ask,' said Jones, burying his face in one hand. 'Just keep filling my glass.'

'Mr Jones doesn't look very happy,' said Emily Mansfield as Colin Dunbar appeared to refill their wine glasses. 'Is there bad news about his health?'

'On the contrary,' said Colin. 'His health is perfect. That heart report was a mistake they made in the doctor's surgery. It was a different V. Jones.'

'Well, that's good, isn't it?' said Oscar.

'For him,' said Colin Dunbar.

Emily Mansfield had stringent reservations about Jones. She thought he looked like one of those men who would tell you their life story if you weren't careful.

But she was offended by Colin Dunbar's reaction to his good news.

'You see what harm your little insurance idea is doing, Oscar?' she said. 'Your friends now want each other dead.'

'I'm not responsible for the cupidity of men,' said Oscar. 'I just thought of an idea, that's all.'

He had too much respect for his wife to get involved in an argument. He always lost them, anyway, and this was his birthday. But he wondered how the protective noises she was making about Jones would survive the news that he had made love to one of his students in a field.

'Jones made love to one of his students in a field,' he said, pausing only fleetingly to consider whether this was an appropriate subject to raise in front of Adrian.

'You're not serious?' said Emily, looking genuinely shocked. 'In a field?'

'The field is the least important aspect of the story,' said Oscar.

'Does Gaynor know?'

'Presumably not,' said Oscar, 'or Colin wouldn't be looking so disappointed tonight.'

'Do you know the girl's name?' asked Adrian, stirring at last at a conversation he could join.

'I don't believe I do,' Oscar told him.

'I bet it was Rosemary Friedland,' said Adrian. 'She does it with everybody.'

'I think we'll drop this subject, if you don't mind,' said Emily, looking disapprovingly at her son. 'Who's for the chocolate roulade? It's got fresh raspberries and cream inside.'

'I'm going to get a bottle of champagne,' said Oscar. 'You're not forty-one every day.'

At the counter Jones took him to one side. 'Colin said you were eavesdropping on a conversation among my students. Can you remember what was said?'

'You bonked a girl in a field and you weren't the first to enjoy her, was the gist of it. I was pretty surprised, Vernon. *In loco parentis* and all that. I know the education system's a shambles, but I didn't know it had come to that.'

'What else did they say? I'm thinking of consequences here, Oscar.'

Oscar Mansfield looked at Jones's troubled face, and a saying about paying for your pleasures in this world flickered across his mind.

'No consequences,' he said. 'They were treating it as a bit of a joke.'

'Some joke,' said Jones miserably.

'What was she like? I haven't had a seventeen-year-old since——'

'I know. Since you were seventeen.'

'Anyway, good news about your health. I'm delighted.' He took a bottle of Cordon Rouge back to the table.

'What was Jones saying?' Emily asked.

'He's a worried man again.'

'And so he bloody ought to be.'

The champagne was opened with minimum spillage as Colin Dunbar arrived with glasses.

'Have one yourself, Colin,' said Oscar.

'Yes,' said Emily. 'Drink to everyone's health.'

When they reached home an hour later, Oscar Mansfield felt pretty good for a man who was now quite definitely embarked on the second half of his life. He poured himself a glass of Amaretto while Emily made herself a coffee.

'The essay!' he said. 'We nearly forgot the essay.'

'I'll get it,' said Adrian. 'I hope you've got a new ten-pound note.'

When Oscar and Emily were sitting down with their respective drinks, he came back into the room and handed Oscar an exercise book that had obviously lain unused for a long time. The essay, written in pencil in a small, neat handwriting, occupied the first three pages of the book. Oscar sat back in his chair and started to read.

On Wednesday afternoon I went for a walk. I saw a ginger cat that was stalking a white butterfly at the side of the road. Most animals kill to eat but cats kill out of boredom. This makes them unattractive creatures in my opinion.

I went into the newsagents and looked at the magazines. They were all about girls, computers or sport, none of which interest me. This was just as well as I didn't have any money anyway.

In the evening I stayed in and watched television with my mother and stepfather. It was a programme about babies. It said a mother will wake up when her own baby cries but not when another baby does. In Russia fathers are not allowed to attend the birth or see the baby until it is a week old.

Perhaps the programme made me dream about my father who doesn't live with us any more. I was in a television studio and a row of girls were dancing on a stage. One of them was my father, and I said 'Come down, Dad. You're not a girl' and he said 'Go away, boy.'

This morning something really interesting happened and I bet Oscar thinks his money has been well spent. I decided to get out my bike and go for a ride to find something to write about. At first I thought that not a lot happens round here. People stand at bus stops, go into shops and take their dogs for a walk. That's about it.

But after half an hour I was cycling near Mr Jones's bungalow and Mrs Wyatt drove up in her Range Rover. What made me interested was the clothes that Mrs Wyatt was wearing. She had a very very short skirt and high heels and looked like one of those tarts in the magazines at the newsagents.

When she went into the house I propped my bike against the hedge and crept up to a side window to get something to write about. It was like a Just William story I read once.

Well, when I got to the window Mrs Wyatt was lying on the sofa and Mr Jones had taken off his trousers. I couldn't see what happened then because Mr Jones lay down with her and the back of the sofa was in the way. After a while they got up and lay on the floor. I couldn't see them then either but in my opinion they were engaging in sexual intercourse.

As I cycled home I wondered whether I could be a detective when I grow up.

I spent this afternoon writing this essay. It has taken me over two hours because I write slowly. I have also had to look up words in the dictionary, like 'stalking' and 'intercourse'.

Today is Oscar's birthday and instead of me buying him a present, he is going to give me ten pounds which is nice.

This essay is 500 words exactly.

'God's teeth!' said Oscar, passing the essay to his wife. 'Jones has turned into a shagging machine!'

'What has he done now?' cried Emily, already appalled.

'Read it! Read it! Read your son's sensational essay.' He turned to Adrian. 'I haven't got a new ten-pound note but I've got a dirty twenty-pound note if you're not too fastidious.'

'That will do nicely,' said Adrian. 'There weren't any mistakes, were there?'

'None that I could see. I like the way you made it exactly five hundred words. You don't like to give anything away, do you?'

Adrian smirked complacently. 'I think you got value for money.'

Emily Mansfield was reading the essay with a

mixture of horror and repugnance. Oscar watched her eyebrows rise and fall as she digested her son's literary effort. When she had finished, she dropped the exercise book on the floor as if it had been contaminated by something harmful.

'He didn't make it up, I suppose?' suggested Oscar hopefully.

'Not a chance,' said Emily emphatically. 'He couldn't make that up if he tried. What are we going to do?'

'Do?' said Oscar. 'Are we called upon to do anything?'

'You can't have a man like that roaming the neighbourhood. Nobody's safe.'

Oscar Mansfield sipped his Amaretto, feeling the need to enter a plea on behalf of his disparaged gender. 'And what about Lavinia Wyatt roaming the neighbourhood in mini-skirt and high heels? She visited him, remember.'

'And the girl student he had sex with at the age of forty-five? Who do we blame there? There seems to be one offender here, common to both stories.'

In discussions of this nature Oscar Mansfield was accustomed to coming second.

'I wish we'd followed your suggestion and got Adrian to paint a picture,' he said, staring at the discarded exercise book on the floor.

II

Any doubts that Julian Wyatt had about selling his house were dispelled with crusty vehemence by the surliest of the bank managers whose reluctant support he had relied upon during the last desperate months.

'Selling your house will restore some credibility to the accounts,' said Hendon, a young and confident man who looked as if he was not long out of college. 'Your profits grow but your debts grow faster.'

'I'm not unaware of that,' said Julian Wyatt. 'It seems to flout all known laws of economics.' He hated being beholden to men who were at least a decade younger than himself more than anything else and found it difficult to exhibit the correct mixture of respect and gratitude.

'Not at all,' said Hendon, running fingers through thick black hair that had not yet receded by as much as a millimetre. 'It's an intrinsic part of the recession and especially prevalent in your business where you have to spend money on a piece of business that you have not yet got and might not ever get. Everybody has to speculate to accumulate but in the advertising world it seems to be taken to dangerous lengths.'

'But when it works the profits are wonderful,' Julian Wyatt felt compelled by fairness to point out.

Hendon lowered his clear blue eyes to the balance sheets on his desk. 'At this stage a fresh problem emerges. Getting the business is one hurdle, getting paid for it afterwards is another.'

'It's not my fault that firms go bust when they owe me money.'

'Indeed not, but it's a factor in our little equation.' Hendon swept the balance sheets to one side as if this seminar was leading him nowhere. 'Put your house on the market, Mr Wyatt, and we'll sustain you while the deal goes through. With cash to spare you'll fight your way through these grim times. In ten years you'll probably be a rich man.'

'But if I don't put my house on the market you wouldn't sustain me?'

'Head Office would never permit it.'

The estate agent was called Harris and he scouted round the premises like a policeman in search of a corpse.

'What sort of price did you have in mind?' he asked.

'Three hundred thousand?'

'There's no such price in the house market. You can have £295,000 or even £299,000 if you like.'

'Are the public really that stupid?' asked Julian Wyatt.

148

'Luckily, yes,' said Harris, standing in the open-plan breakfast room and muttering to himself, 'Beamed ceiling. Adjustable spotlights to ceiling. Twin single and double radiators. What's in the cloakroom?'

'A loo and a sink.'

Harris opened the door. 'Suite of low-level close-coupled WC with wooden seat and wash-hand basin.'

'That's what I said.'

'I'm talking into a tape-recorder,' said Harris, and Julian Wyatt suddenly noticed a wire that ran from a tiny microphone in his hand to a machine in his pocket.

They went upstairs.

'I like the arched window overlooking the garden,' said Harris. 'There's a new law, you know.'

'A new law?' said Julian Wyatt.

'The Property Misdescription Act of 1991. We hardly dare describe anything now in case somebody throws the book at us. Mostly we say 'It deserves to be seen' and leave it to the potential buyer.'

'That must make life easier for you.'

'But harder to sell houses. Do you think I can call that a Gothic-style mahogany-framed window, or will I get into trouble?'

'It sounds accurate enough to me.'

'Well, I'll leave you for a while and measure the rooms. We have to get that dead right, too.'

'I'll wait in the garden,' said Julian Wyatt. 'I've got some phone calls to make.'

'This house has a phone in the garden?'

'No, I've got one in my pocket. Do you think we're going to sell this place easily? What do you think of it?'

'It deserves to be seen,' said Harris.

Returning to college after his half-term break, Jones felt like a man who had spent seven consecutive days on the Big Dipper. The highs and the lows were engraved on his brain. He had peered over the abyss with Dr Bradley, and soared to new heights of confidence on learning about the mistake. He had experienced moments of pleasure with Lavinia Wyatt the memory of which still made his legs tremble, and had then been plunged into fear and despair by the news of his gossiping students.

Today he had no option but to behave as if none of these things had happened, and he diverted his impassive class with tremendous passion, defying them to even think about allowing their thoughts to stray in the direction of cornfields. A barrage of information, interspersed with searching questions, fixed their concentration, and he was helped in this endeavour by the fact that Rosemary Friedland was one of today's absentees.

The message arrived at lunchtime. A secretary intercepted him as he was heading for the canteen, and told him that Hayes would like to see him at two. Hayes was the Head, and the news depressed Jones's appetite to such an extent that he decided to give the canteen a miss and wait with a cigarette among whatever newspapers had been left in the staffroom. At five to two he combed his hair, straightened his tie and walked with a spurious confidence to the Head's austere office.

Hayes was a giant of a man who persisted for some reason in wearing wire-framed National Health glasses which for most of the time he looked over rather than through. He was never seen without his gown.

He beckoned Jones to an isolated seat that was placed in front of his own high desk, behind which he himself sat in a Windsor chair. He said: 'I suppose you know why I've sent for you?'

Jones regarded Hayes as an obdurate bonehead inexplicably promoted far beyond his talents and felt towards him an animus that he struggled to control.

'No idea, Headmaster,' he said.

'It's a girl,' said Hayes. 'A student called Rosemary Friedland.'

'Yes?' said Jones.

Hayes stared across the desk, realising that his hope that he would be spared from going into unpleasant details was quite misplaced.

'Well, the story that went round was that you — how shall I put it? — have had carnal knowledge of her. In a cornfield, apparently. I don't imagine that you're going to deny it. I've spoken to the girl and her account was quite graphic. I've no doubt that she was telling the truth, no doubt at all. I've had to send her home to consider her future.'

Jones, with his plentiful flaws, was rarely lost for

words, but now he could think of nothing to offer. Hayes, seeing the whole burden of this exchange fall upon him, ploughed on.

'I can honestly say, Jones, that I would have been less surprised if the Prime Minister had been arrested for shoplifting, or if the Queen . . .'

'I get your drift, Headmaster,' said Jones as Hayes groped helplessly for some hypothetical Royal misdemeanour. 'You're nonplussed.'

'Indeed.'

'I don't know what I can say.'

'Probably not a lot,' said Hayes, fiddling with papers on his desk. 'I suppose you'll be dismissed. That's not up to me. All I can do is suspend you immediately and report the matter to the governors. As a breach of trust, I can't imagine a more serious offence.'

'Do you mean suspended from now?'

'That's what immediately means, I believe. Without delay or intervention, at once, instantly. English is your subject, Jones.'

'It sounds as if it *was* my subject,' said Jones, standing up.

'Better collect your things.'

The next hour, when Jones tried to recall it afterwards, was vague in his mind, but at the end of it he was sitting on a stool at the bar of the Oasis of Sanity.

'Lager?' said Colin Dunbar.

'Whisky,' said Jones.

'Isn't it a little early for you?'

'Make it a double.'

'Got a date in a haystack?'

'Don't be funny, Colin. Humour's not your forte.'

'My,' said Colin Dunbar, 'we are grouchy today.'

As Jones was his only customer and not in the best of moods, he left him with his whisky and retreated to the comfort of his sitting room where Fay was using the one break she got in the day to watch an old film.

'Where's the palindrome?' he asked.

'Don't call her that, Colin,' said Fay irritably. 'Her name's Hannah.'

'Where is she, anyway?'

'Playing with her friend, Tina. Thank God she finds people to play with after school. We've got little enough time for her, trying to run this place.'

Colin Dunbar could see, with the pain of experience, that the atmosphere here was no better than in the bar. Perhaps it was the wrong time of the month; perhaps the constraints imposed by running the Oasis of Sanity were beginning to affect his wife's nerves. There was indeed something claustrophobic about their life now, but until they produced sufficient profits to hire staff and take time off, he didn't see what he could do about it.

The banging of a glass on the bar outside relieved him of the necessity to fret over this particular quandary, and he went out to find Jones holding aloft his empty glass.

'Did I ever tell you about my grandmother?' he asked.

'Another double?' asked Colin Dunbar, taking the

glass. It was clear to him that one large whisky had produced in Jones the desire to talk.

'Yes, make it a double. It works quicker,' he said.

Colin Dunbar handed him the refilled glass. 'What's this about your grandmother?' he asked.

'She was my father's mother. My mother had been removed from the scene years earlier after a rather embarrassing incident.'

'It sounds more interesting than your grandmother.'

'That's not the story I'm telling. You wouldn't believe it, anyway. This grandmother, my father's mother, was a dour old lady with rigid presbyterian views. One day, when I was twenty, she said to me in her sombre Cumbrian accent, "And what are you doing this weekend, young man?" I told her I was parachuting, which was a craze of the time. She walked out of the room and didn't speak to me again for two years. Nobody knew why, but she was an eccentric old dear and we had learned to live with her little oddities.'

Jones chuckled to himself and drank some whisky.

'Is that the end of the story?' Colin Dunbar asked. 'It seems to lack something.'

'No, listen. We only saw her once or twice a year so two years' silence didn't seem very long. But eventually I was too curious to let it ride. I got her on her own one day and said, "Grandma, why won't you talk to me any more?" "It's because of your hobbies, Vernon," she said. "They disgust me." "Disgust you?" I said. "What hobbies are you talking about?" I was at teachers' training college by then and didn't have any hobbies at all, let alone disgusting ones. "It's not fair, it's not sporting. They don't move fast enough." "Grandma," I said. "What are you talking about?" "Parrot shooting," she said.'

Jones chuckled immoderately at the memory of this, and Colin Dunbar, who could only manage a polite smile, attributed it to the whisky.

'Why are you drinking like this?' he asked.

'My life has taken a turn today and I am marking it with a drink.'

'A turn for the better?'

'For the better? You're talking to Vernon Jones, not Inigo Jones. A turn for the worse. I am no longer a college teacher. For the first time in my life I have joined the great army of unemployed.'

'Oh dear,' said Colin Dunbar, astonished to see that half of the second whisky had already gone. 'Why is that?'

Jones shook his head very slowly. 'I'm not a womaniser, Colin. I've never chased skirt. I've always shown women the respect I expect them to show me.'

'I see,' said Colin. 'They found out about your copulation in the corn.'

Jones had now drunk just enough to find interruptions difficult to handle.

'None of us is immune to temptation,' he said. 'We're flesh and blood. And when nobody has bothered to tempt you for years, you're particularly vulnerable if temptation appears. Along comes a willing girl with white teeth and breasts like footballs and the next

155

thing you know your face is buried in a cornfield and you can't remember where your trousers are.'

'And then you lose your job,' said Colin Dunbar.

'That's apparently the way it goes,' said Jones. 'Fill this glass, will you?'

Colin Dunbar held the glass to the optic, awed by the scale of Jones's downfall.

'What are you going to do?' he asked, but again his words were only background noise to Jones who was wrestling with his own confused thought processes.

'You see the problem, don't you?' he asked.

'Money?' suggested Colin.

'The problem isn't the sacking, although the sacking is bad enough. The problem is explaining the reason for the sacking to Gaynor. It's not the behaviour she expects from her husband.'

'Or from anyone else's husband, I should think,' said Colin Dunbar, confident now that his interjections were reaching no audience.

'At a basic level, it's adultery.'

'And a cornfield is a pretty basic level,' said Colin. 'I think you need a summit meeting with your wife.'

This time the words seemed to have got through. 'Summitry, symmetry, cemetery,' Jones mumbled, putting the glass to his lips. 'I'm not a womaniser.'

'But you imitate one very convincingly,' said Colin Dunbar. 'What you did, Vernon, was wrong. With a teenage student. Blimey! I can't condone it. My daughter might be a student there one day.' He was glad to get this off his chest without offending a regular customer who obviously wasn't listening.

'I'm not a womaniser, but none of us is immune to temptation.'

Colin Dunbar was familiar with the loop syndrome in drunk customers' conversations, and he recognised this as the point where he came in. It was time to go out and take a shower before the evening business made escape impossible.

'Don't drink that too quickly. I'll be back in a minute. If a customer comes in, call for Fay.'

'Better fill it again before you go.'

When Colin Dunbar had gone, Jones tried to work out his strategy for dealing with today's disastrous news, the crucial effect of which centred more and more on his wife. The enthusiasm that Gaynor had shown for him in the recent past had not been so rapturous that their legally-sanctioned relationship could easily survive today's news from the college, and then he would not only have no job, but also no wife, no home and, presently, no money. Terrible premonitions coursed through his entire system, temporarily immobilising different parts of his body. For a few moments he couldn't even persuade his hand to pick up his whisky, a deprivation that seemed cruelly excessive after the blow he had suffered.

The loss of his job was not something that he could conceal, but he tried to envisage a way in which he could keep from his wife the reason for it. Staff cuts, inter-departmental rivalry, or a clash of personalities with the demented fool they referred to as Headmaster all carried a scintilla of credibility, but Gaynor didn't live in a bubble — she went out and met people, and people talked. Soon the story of the lecherous lecturer would be part of local folklore.

He rocked backwards and forwards on his stool, relaxing sufficiently to regain his hold on the whisky which he drank in one go to avoid any involuntary abstinence if his hand let him down again. But now he was faced with an empty glass and he looked at it as if it had betrayed him.

In the long dry minutes before Colin Dunbar returned, he caught a glimpse of a plan: he would tell his wife that he had been wrongly accused. The moral climate was on his side. There were kids around now who invented the most terrible stories to liven up their drab lives. Girls went to police stations and described in intricate detail rapes that had never taken place. It would all help Gaynor to believe his side of the story, and he had another undeniable fact in his favour: it would be much easier for Gaynor to believe that Jones had not had intercourse, rather than that he had.

Marginally reassured by this he lifted his glass to bang the counter, but at that moment Colin Dunbar returned refreshed, in a clean white shirt.

'Tell her they've got it wrong,' he said. 'Say you've been accused of something you didn't do.'

'Just what I was thinking,' said Jones, with his first smile of the afternoon.

'I thought of it in the shower. I should think Gaynor

would find it much easier to believe you are innocent than guilty, anyway. You're hardly Tom Cruise.'

'No need to be rude, Colin, old bean. We've cracked it. Now just fill this receptacle up.'

Colin Dunbar took the glass and filled it. 'Are you driving?' he asked.

'Never drive in a bar,' Jones said. 'Find the furniture gets in the way.' He seemed to have moved to phase two in the drinker's odyssey, where silly jokes replace sullen introspection.

'And don't drive home, either,' said Colin. 'The police look out for people like you and you don't want a huge fine now you've lost your job.'

'If I didn't know you better, Colin, I'd say you were turning into a bit of an old woman,' said Jones, draining his whisky. 'But you're quite right. I ought to be getting home while I'm still conscious. Driving's bloody hazardous when you're sound asleep.'

He stood up and steadied himself with a hand on the counter. His bloodshot eyes gazed at Colin Dunbar but seemed to be focused on some point beyond him. 'Life of leisure starts today,' he said.

Colin Dunbar came round from behind the counter and wondered how he could prevent Jones from getting into his car.

'Stay and have a black coffee,' he suggested.

'Oblivion looms,' said Jones. 'No time for coffee.'

He walked out of the bar almost normally and Colin Dunbar followed him to the door. Oscar Mansfield was just driving into the front car park in his BMW, arriving promptly for his early evening drink. He parked his car in his usual place and began walking across the car park as Jones started the engine of his old Vauxhall.

Sitting in the car he didn't feel too bad. It was a short journey on quiet roads and he should be able to reach home without any mishaps. He found reverse, put his foot on the accelerator and shot backwards rather faster than he had expected. There was an unusual noise, a bump of some sort, and the rear of the car went up as the wheel went over an obstacle that he hadn't seen.

He spoke to Colin Dunbar through his open window.

'What was that?'

But Colin Dunbar was running towards him and shouting, 'You've hit Oscar!'

'Oscar?' said Jones. 'Where did he come from?'

He turned off his engine and climbed with difficulty from the Vauxhall.

Oscar Mansfield was lying on his back underneath the car. His eyes were shut and the message on his shirt said *Free the Grecian 2000*.

'What do we do now?' asked Jones, surveying a situation of baffling complexity. 'Is he dead?'

'Don't touch him,' shouted Colin Dunbar, who was running back towards the bar. 'I'll phone an ambulance.'

Jones bent down and peered beneath the Vauxhall.

'Oscar, old mate, what are you doing there?' he asked.

But Oscar Mansfield lay motionless on the ground, a tyre mark over one leg and blood running down his face.

'Oscar, old mate,' said Jones, 'what do you want to drink?'

12

It was some time before Gaynor Jones was able to unravel the events of the day and assemble them in an order that made sense to her. Her husband had arrived home white-faced, looking as if wild dogs were at his heels, tripped over the step and, after a prolonged visit to the lavatory, collapsed groaning into an armchair from which he looked as if he might never rise again.

The shock, or the walk home, or the regurgitant stopover in the bathroom, had sobered him sufficiently for a degree of coherence to appear, but he was now suffering from memory gaps that required both patience and interrogative skills from his wife.

She sat on the sofa opposite him, appraising the wreckage that he had become, and slowly put together a picture of his day. He had been suspended after a girl had falsely accused him of an act of indecency, had a few drinks in an understandable state of agitation, and accidentally knocked Oscar Mansfield over when he tried to leave in his car. Oscar, alive but unconscious, had been taken to hospital with head injuries and a suspected broken leg, and Vernon had stumbled home, distraught and demoralised. Gaynor Jones didn't know where to start.

'Didn't the police breathalyse you?' she asked.

'They couldn't,' said Jones. 'By the time they got there I'd gone back into the bar and had a few more.'

'Will they prosecute?'

'Who knows? They made notes. Can they prosecute for something that happens in a car park? It wasn't on the public highway, was it?'

'This girl,' said Gaynor. 'Is she mad?'

'Evidently,' said Jones.

The possibility that Jones had had intercourse with anybody, let alone one of his own students, did not enter his wife's mind. In her opinion, rampant sexuality was the only fault he didn't have, and the only one which in rare moments she might have welcomed. She hugged her knees on the sofa and stared at her disconsolate husband.

'What about the National Union of Teachers, or whatever your militant fundamentalists are called. Won't they stand up for you?'

'A few token gestures, I expect. The power of the unions these days is sadly over-estimated.'

Jones sat back in the armchair wondering whether to go to bed or throw up. Of the day's various disasters, it was the sanguinary joust in the car park that lingered with him now. He didn't like Oscar Mansfield's appearance when he was stretched out beneath the Vauxhall Viva. He looked like a man already dead, and it was hard to believe that if he survived he would ever be his normal, robust self again. Just picturing his death-like face made Jones feel queasy, and he struggled to direct his thoughts elsewhere. Unfortunately his brain was not amenable to suggestion, and he sat there glassy-eyed with a dry tongue that felt slightly larger than his foot.

Examining his torpid condition Gaynor Jones experienced feelings of bewilderment that she had never known before. For a man whose uneventful progress through life had been a dismally reliable source of tedium and ennui to suddenly find himself enmeshed in a scandal that involved sex, drink and the police was so weird and so unlike him that she couldn't find the words that the situation warranted.

'This indecency,' she said eventually. 'What do they allege you did?'

'Fondled her breasts,' said Jones promptly. He had heard of these things happening in the cloistered corridors of the college, and felt that it fitted perfectly the allegation that his wife was discussing.

'But you would never do something like that,' his wife remarked sadly. 'For God's sake, you don't even look at beautiful women in the street.'

'Tell *them*,' said Jones. 'The girl is obviously out to get me. I probably gave her bad marks in some test.'

'And why should Hayes believe her and not you?'

'Because Hayes is a cretin who shouldn't be allowed out on his own.'

He leaned back in his chair, no longer able to keep his eyes open.

'I think I'll go to bed,' he said. 'Tomorrow I'll be able to think clearly.'

But when he woke up the following morning his head throbbed with a virulence that had him pleading for Veganin. Gaynor arrived at his bedside with tablets and a glass of water.

'You must go to see Emily,' he said with his eyes shut. 'Explain, apologise, find out how he is. Tell her I'll visit the hospital this afternoon.' He opened his eyes long enough to swallow the tablets and then sank gratefully back on the pillow.

'And I've got to walk to the Oasis to get the car?'

'I'm afraid you have.'

Emily Mansfield was on the phone to the hospital when Gaynor Jones arrived at Rose Cottage in the Vauxhall. The door was opened by Adrian, who stared at her in disgust.

'How's Oscar?' she asked, when no invitation to come in was offered.

'Bad,' said Adrian. 'He's got to have a brain scan.'

'I'm so sorry,' said Gaynor. 'Is your mother in?'

'She's on the phone,' said Adrian. 'I suppose it was all that sex with Mrs Wyatt that affected your husband's driving?'

'What?' said Gaynor, confused.

Emily Mansfield appeared looking grim.

'Come in,' she said. 'What a terrible business this is.'

Gaynor Jones followed her through to the kitchen where she was making coffee.

'He had a bad night and they're going to give him a brain scan,' said Emily Mansfield. 'They've got to find out what the damage is. Sit down. I'll make you coffee.'

'Vernon is distraught,' said Gaynor. 'He asked me to come round to see how Oscar is. He wants to visit him in hospital later on.'

'He was drunk, I gather,' said Emily Mansfield. 'Oscar's not a good age to be knocked about like that.'

'It's terrible,' said Gaynor. 'I don't know what to say. Apologies are hardly adequate. But it's so unlike Vernon.'

'Vernon is not a popular name in this house today. I hear he's been sacked?'

'Suspended,' said Gaynor, accepting a coffee. 'He's obviously innocent.'

She looked up, disturbed at the silence which followed this assertion. Did Emily Mansfield believe that her husband molested girls? She drank her coffee, embarrassed by this break in the conversation, and then she remembered what Adrian had said at the door.

'Your son made a curious remark to me just now,' she said.

'Curious?' said Emily Mansfield.

'Something about Vernon having sex with Lavinia Wyatt.'

'He shouldn't have mentioned that. I'm afraid that

Adrian is upset by what happened last night. He's very fond of Oscar in his way.'

'What do you mean — he shouldn't have mentioned it?' asked Gaynor. 'Are you suggesting that it's true?'

'It is true, Gaynor. I wouldn't put it past him to have had a couple of students as well. Dissolute, I believe, is the word.'

Gaynor Jones put down her coffee. 'Hang on a minute, Emily,' she said. 'I can understand your anger, but to pretend that Vernon is some kind of sex maniac is obviously ridiculous.'

Emily Mansfield paused, but was just angry enough to continue: 'Vernon had sex with Lavinia Wyatt, Gaynor. Don't doubt it. Adrian watched them through a window. They did it on a sofa, then they did it on the floor.'

'I don't believe it.'

'Please yourself.'

'Do you believe it?'

'I know it to be true.'

'Because Adrian said so?'

'Yes, Gaynor. Because Adrian said so. Oscar paid him some money to write an essay about what he did and saw over twenty-four hours. Adrian was cycling by your place when Lavinia drove up in the Range Rover in a mini-skirt. It aroused his interest and, distasteful though it is to admit it, he peered through the window. It was last Thursday. I expect you were playing tennis.'

'No, I was in London,' said Gaynor, who believed it

now. 'My God! With Lavinia Wyatt! What does she need Vernon for? She's already got two lovers that I know of.'

'My dear girl,' said Emily Mansfield, 'the human is the most evil creature on earth, scheming, deceitful, vicious, capable of depths of depravity that are quite unknown in the animal kingdom. I'd have thought you'd have known that.'

But Gaynor Jones was now dabbing her eyes with a pink handkerchief, horror-stricken by the information coming her way, and she was in no mood for a cerebral chat about the frailties of human behaviour. Her first reaction was remorse at the naivety that had let her believe her husband. Her second was more pragmatic, and Emily Mansfield could see that the tears, if there had been tears, were a short-lived phenomenon.

'I'll ditch the sod,' she said. 'I'll screw the bastard for every penny he's got.'

'That's the spirit,' said Emily Mansfield, encouraged. 'More coffee?'

'I'll take him to the cleaners, I'll eviscerate the moron. I'll have him pleading for mercy in a pool of blood.'

'You've got the idea,' said Emily Mansfield. 'And when you split, be sure to take his car. We'll all be a lot safer.'

Gaynor Jones sat at the kitchen table considering this vigorous programme of revenge with a tight smile on her lips. 'For God's sake,' she said, 'anyone would think being married to him was fun!'

'I should think Vernon is to fun what the Vénus de

Milo is to arm-wrestling,' said Emily. 'It's always best to leave them when they lose their jobs. The last good reason for putting up with them has disappeared, and they've ceased to be of any earthly use.'

'You sound like one of the pioneers of Women's Lib, Emily,' said Gaynor, holding up her empty coffee cup.

Emily Mansfield briskly refilled it. 'Not at all. Oscar is a wonderful man and he's been truly kind. But my first marriage gave me a slightly cynical view of the wedlock business. I hadn't planned on being married to a woman.'

'It must have been awful.'

'It wasn't a lot of laughs, but that's men for you. I'll write a letter about them one of these days. The mystery of men.'

Gaynor Jones drank her second coffee and contemplated a life without Vernon. Apart from the financial problems that would no doubt accompany her, it was a vista of unblemished happiness. And as the financial problems would arise anyway, now that her husband had fallen off his dreary academic perch, an immediate separation was an option with no discernible drawback. She stood up to go.

'Tell Oscar how sorry I am,' she said. 'If there's anything I can take him, please let me know.'

'Probably best if Vernon stays away,' said Emily Mansfield, collecting cups. 'Give Oscar time to recover his sense of humour.'

Driving away in a strange mood of exhilaration, Gaynor Jones was able to survive for some time on the repugnance she felt towards her husband, with his deceit and adulterous behaviour. She seemed to be carried along on the stimulus of her disgust. But after a few miles, when the novelty of her anger began to pall, her thoughts turned to Lavinia Wyatt.

The fact that she had visited the Jones's bungalow suggested that she was the prime mover in what had occurred. She had certainly shown a crude disregard for Gaynor's interests and feelings.

She drove on until she reached the Post Office and then parked the Vauxhall and went to look for a telephone.

At the offices of Wyatt Promotions a small celebration was taking place. It wasn't a champagne celebration – those were reserved for pieces of business that were expected to yield a six-figure profit. But several bottles of white wine were being passed round in a brief ceremony of self-congratulation. A contract had been signed with a soup manufacturer who was exhibiting at the National Exhibition Centre. Wyatt Promotions, having originally bid to produce the brochures and leaflets, had now been given the whole job. They would design and make the stand, organise the display and provide girls with giveaways for passing punters. The cost to the soup manufacturer would be £120,000 and Wyatt Promotions should show a profit of about £35,000 on the week.

Julian Wyatt slapped backs, sipped wine and moved among his staff exuding relief. The deal, and the prospective house sale, gave a rosier glow to his future. But by the time that he had returned to his desk, the documentary evidence of his problems lay all round him.

He was now getting daily bank statements, an ominous development that said all there was to say about his shaky situation. He had endured a little lecture earlier that morning from one of his friendlier bank managers.

'You're growing too fast,' he said. 'It's very danger- ous for a new business.'

'I always imagined growing was healthy,' said Julian Wyatt, surprised to be rebuked for what he regarded as a small corner of success.

'Not for new businesses. You need borrowed cash to pay for it.'

It was true. In the last six months he had needed an additional quarter of a million from the banks in working capital to fund his growth. He was turning over £300,000 a month but the bills from his various suppliers alone were £150,000. Worst of all, instead of lunching three or four times a week with potential clients in the quest for business he had to cut down to one lunch a week as more time was needed to keep a nervous eye on his faltering cash flow.

He was sitting at his desk considering this when the phone rang. Any call that got past the vetting talents of Avis, his secretary, was important and he picked it up immediately, bracing himself for demands for money or feeble explanations about why he was not going to get some this month that he was owed.

'It's Gaynor Jones,' said a voice he hardly recognised.

'Gaynor?' said Julian Wyatt, whose mind was in a different world.

'I thought I should ring you,' said Gaynor.

'What is it, Gaynor?' A hint of impatience at the idea of a social call intruding on his many preoccupations in this office fizzled down the line.

'It's about your wife,' said Gaynor. 'I thought you should know.'

'Lavinia? What's happened to her?'

'She's been getting laid,' said Gaynor. 'By my husband, oddly enough.'

'Don't pull my leg, Gaynor. I'm a busy man.'

'It's true, Julian. They've been bonking like alley cats in the bungalow. I'm leaving him today.'

Julian Wyatt went purple, then crimson and then a sort of vermilion.

'With Jones?' he asked finally in a tone of voice which still held out the possibility of a joke.

'He's capable of sex, Julian. It's a subject that I'm qualified to speak on. But she's also got a builder boyfriend, in case you didn't know.'

Julian Wyatt was accustomed to handling crises at this desk. For much of his life he did little else. He struggled to find the important question.

'What grounds have you got for saying this, Gaynor?' he asked.

'I was given the information by Emily Mansfield. Apparently Adrian watched it all going on through our window. His stepfather had encouraged him to write an essay about what he did and saw during the course of twenty-four hours.'

'And he saw that?'

'It's in his essay. They did it on the sofa, then they did it on the floor.'

'Thanks for ringing, Gaynor.'

When he had replaced the phone, Julian Wyatt sat without moving for some time. He had always harboured suspicions about his wife but had never discovered any evidence to justify them. She had the perky self-confidence of the frequently laid when he was at his most dormant, a paradox that he had often noticed and fretted over. On one occasion she had mysteriously acquired an engraved gemstone, an intaglio that looked much more like a lover's gift than an impulse purchase of her own.

For several moments he sat there, rolling this new catastrophe round in his mind. For months now he had no sooner got his brain focused on one problem than another arrived to knock the first one unsolved from his thoughts. But this one stuck, even surviving the interruption of his secretary who came in to tell him that Flounders & Proudlock wanted money.

'Fuck Flounders & Proudlock, Avis,' he said calmly. 'I have a problem at home.'

'So have I,' said Avis. 'He's called Denis.'

'He's not being unfaithful to you, is he?'

'Unfaithful? Good God, no,' said Avis, and went out to tell everyone that Julian's wife was having it off with somebody and the staff should keep out of his way. Then she returned to her desk and called Flounders & Proudlock to tell them that Julian would be in touch as soon as he had finished a board meeting. But half an hour later when she went to his office he had gone.

Jones crept from his bed with a nervous fragility that reached every corner of his body. Moving cautiously like a cat he established that the tablets had worked and the headache had gone, but the rest of him seemed to be promising that he would vomit or expire in the very near future. But throwing water over his face in the bathroom he detected the beginning of a revival, and by the time he had dressed and reached the kitchen he could see that he was not going to escape the future quite so easily. He was about to make a very black coffee when there was a knock at the front door.

He approached it with misgiving, a doubt that was thoroughly vindicated directly he opened the door. A police sergeant stood smiling apologetically on the mat.

'Mr Jones? It's about the accident last night,' he said. His hands were clasped together in front of him in a signal of relaxed confidence.

'Come in,' said Jones, feeling the nausea return.

When he was settled comfortably in an armchair and had produced notebook and pencil, the sergeant studied Jones for some time as if he was trying to gauge the creature he was dealing with.

'As I understand it,' he began, 'you hit Mr Mansfield when you were reversing your car?'

'I'm afraid so,' said Jones. He seemed to recollect discussing the subject with two policemen last night and found the prospect of further questions disturbing.

'You'd been drinking, of course, but there's not much we can do about that now.'

'So how can I help you, sergeant?' Jones asked, relieved. 'Am I to be hauled before the court?'

'It seems unlikely, all things considered,' said the policeman. 'But Mr Mansfield may want to pursue you in the civil court.'

'My insurance will pay whatever compensation he deserves,' said Jones, beginning to feel more hopeful about the whole business.

'Ah,' said the policeman, brightening up. 'Insurance. This is why I'm here. It's a most unusual case.'

'Unusual?'

'Yes. I understand there was an insurance scheme under which you would benefit from Mr Mansfield's death?'

'What?' said Jones, sitting up.

'Thirty-three grand for you if Mr Mansfield croaks apparently. He's not at all well, I hear, this morning.'

'Are you suggesting— ?' Jones began.

'Mr Jones, I never suggest anything. I deal in facts. I'm asking you questions to which I need answers. Is it the case that you benefit financially from Mr Mansfield's death?'

'Well, put like that, yes.'

'How else can it be put?'

'There are four of us in a joint insurance scheme and we would all benefit from the death of any of the other three. It's quite legal.'

'And you and Mr Mansfield are in this joint scheme?'

Jones nodded unhappily.

'So you would benefit from Mr Mansfield's death?'

'As he would benefit from mine.'

'Unfortunately,' said the police sergeant, 'it wasn't Mr Mansfield who hit you with his car. If it were, we'd be talking to him now.'

Jones struggled to get a grip on himself.

'Sergeant, I resent the implication of your questions more than I can say. The idea that I would try to kill anybody for anything is offensive and absurd. I'm a law-abiding citizen without the slightest stain on my character.'

The sergeant looked up at him as Jones made this passionate declaration of innocence, and then said as if he hadn't been listening: 'I understand you're suspended from the local college over allegations of sexual offences with a young girl student?'

'Jesus,' said Jones.

'It was you who mentioned stains on character, Mr Jones. You're suspended, are you not?'

'Suspended, but innocent.'

'We're all innocent until we're proved guilty, so they tell us. What about this insurance scheme?'

Jones recalled Oscar's idea and how they had all agreed to take part.

The sergeant frowned. 'The idea of people standing to gain from someone else's death is discouraged unless it's family,' he said. 'That's probably why most murders are family affairs.'

'However, it's legal,' said Jones.

'How are your finances?' the sergeant asked, fixing Jones with a gaze that seemed to skewer him to the chair. 'No money problems?'

My God, thought Jones. Now the man is looking for a motive for the attempted murder that he imagines took place. He crossed his legs and tried to look relaxed.

'None at all. I'm a salaried employee at the college. We live quite frugally, all things considered.'

'You *were* a salaried employee. Any debts?'

'A small mortgage. A few credit-card debts at this time of the month. Nothing important.' The sergeant wrote in his notebook, a sight which Jones did not find reassuring. 'You're wasting your time, sergeant. Oscar is one of my closest friends and it was a terrible accident.'

'Maybe,' said the sergeant. 'Maybe. But if your close friend Oscar dies, the whole thing is going to look very different, isn't it?'

'Die?' said Jones. 'He's not going to die, is he?'

'Head injuries are funny things,' said the policeman, tucking his notebook into his pocket. 'Even the doctors don't know what's going on in there half the time.'

Jones's consternation at this suggestion was only partly mitigated by the retirement of the notebook. Every new development in his life seemed to be more disastrous than the previous one, and he wondered what else the world could throw at him. But this ordeal, at least, was over for the sergeant was standing up.

'I'll be going then, Mr Jones, but I expect we'll be in touch.'

'I'll be here if you want me,' said Jones. 'I'm not going anywhere.'

'That's good. Keep your fingers crossed for Mr Mansfield.'

Gaynor arrived home in the Vauxhall as he was seeing the policeman out. She showed no curiosity about the reason for his visit and the expression on her face conveyed with luminous clarity that no favourable adjustment to his misery quotient was imminent. He stood at the door as she swept silently past him and into the bedroom.

The next time he saw her she was carrying suit-cases.

'How's Oscar?' he asked.

'How's Lavinia?'

'Lavinia? How would I know? What's the news on Oscar?'

Gaynor Jones dropped the suitcases by the front door and turned to face him, hands on hips.

'Listen, you disgusting and decrepit little shit, I know all about your affair with Mrs Wyatt and I'm off. I've had more than enough of life as Mrs Jones. You'll be hearing from my solicitors about my proceeds from the sale of this miserable bungalow and several other little things as well.'

179

Jones reeled back and leant against the wall, doubtful whether he could withstand any more bad news.

'Where are you going?' he asked.

'To my mother initially. It won't be fun but any-where's better than here. I suppose the student was telling the truth as well?'

Jones slid down the wall and sat on the floor with his head in his hands. 'We're married, Gaynor,' he said.

'A mistake I propose to rectify,' said Gaynor Jones, enjoying this belated retribution for the tedious years she had spent with her husband. 'I see a dozen couples every day who look as if they are wondering how the hell they managed to get tied up together. Well, I'm going to do something about it.'

There was a time when Jones might have heard this news with a measure of equanimity, but after what had happened to him in the last twenty-four hours it was one shock too many. He had lost his job, he was about to lose his wife and his home, and if the police sergeant had his way he would soon be losing his freedom. He sat on the floor, unable to speak, while his wife disappeared to collect those things that she was going to take with her. Ornaments, small pieces of furniture, a clock, two lamps and a portable television were carried through the front door, and it dawned on Jones, squatting in abject defeat on the floor, that he was going to lose his car as well.

He didn't move. He didn't speak. He sat as if frozen against the wall. As his wife passed him for the last time, her arms laden with bed linen, she paused and told him: 'Don't visit Oscar. That's a request from Emily.'

The door slammed, and he listened to the car start and drive away. It was still some time before he got to his feet, and when he did it was to walk no further than to an armchair. His mouth was dry: he still hadn't eaten or drunk today, and he hadn't the energy to look for anything. He felt numb.

For two hours he sat in the chair, waiting for his brain to start working. When it did, the future became clear: it consisted exclusively of hell and he knew what he had to do. He would collect a video from the local shop and hide from the world this evening. Tomorrow, when he had recovered sufficiently to write a couple of thoughtful letters, he would do what he had always known he would do one day — kill himself.

13

Lavinia Wyatt returned from an invigorating hour on the tennis court to discover her husband crouched over a bottle of Chivas Regal in the conservatory. There were two reasons why this discovery produced in her a flutter of alarm. First, work never allowed Julian to reach home this early; secondly, he did not drink whisky.

She said, 'Hallo, darling. Are you sick?'

Julian Wyatt looked up at her brief white tennis shorts and her brown thighs and thought, You treacherous cow.

'Yeah, I'm sick,' he said, pouring himself a drink. 'I'm sick of you.' He sipped the Chivas Regal and looked at the expression on his wife's face. It was not one that he had seen before. Pain, incredulity and anger merged to give her eyes a diamond shape.

'I think I'd better sit down,' she said, sinking into one of the conservatory's bamboo chairs. 'What's this all about, Julian?'

Julian Wyatt remembered finding this girl at a dinner party in Oxford where her bright spirits and seductive charm ruptured male friendships that had survived for years. Elbows were used in the struggle to bask in her glow. He'd carried her off with pride, and he had been carrying her ever since. His naive impetuosity had blinded him to the financial burden that he was taking on. It had to be the right detached period house, the Range Rover, the public school for their son. He had to buy her Italian knickers that cost £55. Her profligacy was matched by a squeamishness that he found neurotic: she had never used a public toilet in her life.

Glimpsing an end to these onerous obligations, he answered, 'It's about Jones.'

The name tolled like the clang of doom in her heart but her racing mind said: deny, lie, prevaricate. Instinctively she assumed an expression of total mystification. 'Jones? What about Jones?'

'I was hoping you'd tell me,' said Julian Wyatt, drinking more whisky. 'Good in bed, is he?'

Lavinia placed a hand on each knee. 'Julian, what are you talking about?'

'Lavinia, you know very well what I'm talking about. Incredible as it seems to me, you've been screwing Vernon Jones.'

Lavinia Wyatt deflected this with practised disdain. 'That's the most offensive and ridiculous suggestion I've heard for a long time. How much whisky have you had?'

'You were seen, Lavinia. *In flagrante delicto.*'

'Oh, really?' she replied, feeling nervous now. 'And who has been spreading these lies?'

'The Mansfield boy watched it through the window. You did it on the sofa and then you did it on the floor. I must say your taste in men has gone down the tubes.'

The veneer of outrage and indignation began to crumble when Lavinia Wyatt considered what her husband had said. He knew too much for her denials to sound anything but hollow.

He studied her with simmering malevolence. He still had the builder boyfriend to lob into the fray, although somehow that didn't seem so important. He might even have forgiven her that, if no one else knew about it. The demands and worries of work had made him a poor husband. But to do it with Jones who was somehow at the centre of his social life was a humiliation that he was not going to accept.

His wife, he realised, was crying.

'I did it for you,' she said between sobs.

'You screwed Jones for me? That's bloody civil of you, Lavinia.'

'You needed money.'

Julian Wyatt put down his whisky and sat up. 'Do you mean Jones was paying you?'

'Paying me? No. I've been bonking him rotten in the hope that he'd snuff it.'

Julian Wyatt considered this information with a horror that he could not match to any words. He stared at his wife, awaiting an explanation.

'The insurance,' she said. 'He had a heart complaint

and Gaynor said sexual excitement would kill him. You would have got thirty-three grand from your daft insurance scheme.'

'Are you telling me that you were trying to kill him?'

Julian Wyatt could hardly believe the words that were coming out of his own mouth, let alone his wife's.

'He would have died happy,' said Lavinia Wyatt, burying her face in a silk handkerchief that she had taken to the tennis court to mop up sweat.

Julian Wyatt stood up and abandoned his drink. 'I've heard enough,' he said. 'Rather more than enough, actually. I'm moving out today.'

Lavinia looked up.

'Where are you going?'

'Who knows? Who cares? I'm sure as hell not staying in this house.'

'What about Gavin?'

'He doesn't want us. He's going to Australia,' said Julian Wyatt, marching out of the conservatory.

'I'm married to a homicidal nymphomaniac,' he told Colin Dunbar in the Oasis of Sanity half an hour later. 'She's been trying to bonk Jones to death.'

'You'd have to be pretty desperate for money to have intercourse with Vernon,' Colin Dunbar suggested. 'I suppose she was trying to help.'

'Help?' said Julian Wyatt incredulously. 'If she wanted to help she could have got a job. That, I believe, is what most women would have done.'

186

'But they wouldn't earn thirty-three grand in a couple of hours, would they, kid?'

'My God,' said Julian Wyatt. 'You're as corrupt as she is.'

'What are you going to do?'

'Move in here. Have you any rooms?'

'Ah,' said Colin Dunbar. 'Business! You can have bed and breakfast for fifteen a night.'

By the time that Julian Wyatt had carried what possessions he needed from the Range Rover to a spacious bedroom with *en suite* bathroom on the first floor of the Oasis of Sanity, he had calmed down enough to sit at the bar and drink a slow lager. The Chivas Regal had removed the desire for his usual orange juice.

'Did you hear what happened here last night?' Colin Dunbar asked him.

'I must have missed that,' said Julian Wyatt. 'I've had a rather fraught day.'

The story that Colin Dunbar related eased his pain. Jones sacked in disgrace represented good news today and helped to alleviate the distress that he was suffering. He had the sublime feeling that there was justice out there somewhere, and some invisible figure in a horse-hair wig was determined to see that it was administered. The news of Oscar Mansfield, however, was not so good.

'He's had a brain scan,' said Colin.

'Did they find it?' asked Julian.

'Concussion is a funny thing. Perhaps your thirty-three grand will come from another source.'

'I'm beginning to think that Oscar's scheme is bringing out the worst in people,' said Julian Wyatt. 'Have you seen Jones today?'

'He's out of work, isn't he? He can't afford my prices.'

'He's probably shot himself by now. He was pretty suicidal when everything was going well.'

'I hope not,' said Colin Dunbar. 'The insurance would never pay up if he kills himself that quickly.'

A naked man lay on his back, his tongue flicking wistfully at an erect nipple that hung above him. The nipple belonged to a toothy blonde who was herself receiving urgent attention from a second man who was above and behind her. What gratification was being enjoyed by any of them was indicated by peculiar lip distortions, as if the mouth was engaged in combat with a particularly intractable toffee.

Slumped on his sofa, Jones stared boggle-eyed at the heaving buttocks on his television screen. If this was the BBC, it had clearly gone further down the dismal road to vulgar popularisation than even he, with his innate pessimism, had ever predicted.

The scene cut abruptly to two naked women who were drying each other with towels. It wasn't clear why they couldn't dry themselves, nor indeed how they had got wet, but the towelling process seemed to excite them both and suddenly one of them, a dyed blonde with pubic hair made orange by the poor quality of the colour, was on her knees licking the other one's bottom.

Jones gaped in stupefaction at this mélange of jiggling breasts, anguished faces and restless tongues, and wondered to which inferno his sins had brought him. At this time of day he should be watching the nine o'clock news with solemn journalists delivering reports from Downing Street or the gates of Buckingham Palace which they could just as easily have presented in the studio.

He realised that he had fallen asleep, but waking up fast he remembered that he had gone out to rent a video. He thought that he had picked up *Sunset Boulevard* but he saw now that this video was called *Sunny After Dark*. Even his eyes were betraying him.

The eyes that filled the screen stared wildly, the mouths opened and shut like the mouths of fish, women played with their own breasts, jaded, talentless women who didn't even have the bodies that their sad trade demanded. It was a video that he felt like watching from behind the sofa, as he had watched horror films as a boy, and he switched it off. He knew now where sex led and this was no way to spend your last evening on earth.

He fetched a beer from the fridge and some writing paper from his desk and then sat down again in the same seat. He should write to his sister, a woman so much older than him that they had hardly got to know each other, but she was his only surviving close relation and some message seemed to be needed. A valedictory note to the regulars at the Oasis of Sanity might show a certain panache but he wasn't sure he was up to it, particularly as one of the recipients would be Julian Wyatt. He drank some beer and took the top off his Pentel pen.

My dear Agnes, he wrote, and then stopped for another drink. His sister, a humourless spinster who ran a craft centre in the north where she spent her spare time pursuing recreant Tory voters with a relentless vigour that demoralised her opponents, would be surprised to hear from him. For years their only contact had been an impassive exchange of Christmas cards, and he couldn't remember the last time they had met. Given the disparity in their ages it was unlikely that a close relationship would ever have developed, and the business over their mother finally extinguished whatever chances there had been for retaining loving family links.

But he needed to write to her now, to leave some sort of explanation. Even a lady as cold as Agnes would surely be moved in some way by her brother's suicide, and curious about the reasons which lay behind it.

My Dear Agnes, I imagine that you will be surprised to hear from me after all this time. Do not reach for your pen — I am not about to embark on a lengthy correspondence. Indeed, this letter won't even require a reply.

He sipped his beer and stared at the dead screen of the television. Tomorrow morning, he thought, he would chuck the video out. There was no justi-fication for returning it and prolonging the existence of such trash.

My life, he wrote, *has not panned out in the way I hoped when I left teacher training college with the future before me. I was sustained then by dreams and ambitions that have been cruelly treated by the fleeting years.*

He paused and drank more beer. He didn't want to get too lyrical: the demented old bat would be too busy spinning wool, turning wood, and making baskets to appreciate it anyway.

Recently, he wrote, *I have endured a series of misfortunes which would make the experiences of Candide look like an everyday package holiday. I have lost my job and Gaynor has left me. There are other complications in my life that I won't bore you with. Suffice it to say that I feel too old to fight them. I no longer have the spirit and the stamina of the young people I teach every day, and my inclination now is to lie down and let it all roll over me. I have therefore decided —*

He paused again, uncertain where this sentence was going. *To bring things to a close? To end it all? To top myself? To commit suicide? To do myself in? To go to a better place?* The language of suicide seemed unnecessarily melodramatic.

He put down his pen and picked up his beer. Perhaps he wouldn't write to his sister after all. Given the interest that she had shown in his life over the last twenty years, she was hardly going to miss him.

The removal of this duty left him with one final problem: which method of suicide to choose.

14

When Jones was four years old, his mother had thrown him over a cliff.

The opinion among those few people to whom he subsequently confided this story was that his mother had probably grown tired of his mournful demeanour and his shortfall in the area of *joie de vivre*, and imagined that she was performing some service for the world at large. Jones saw this reaction in his listeners and stopped relating the story. It was the embarrassing incident that he had refused to pass on to Colin Dunbar.

The boy's screaming descent to certain death ended in the top of a tree that grew on the side of the cliff. Beyond a few scratches he was unhurt. It was his mother who was taken to hospital and he never saw her again.

In the years that followed, Jones often thought that a halfway competent psychiatrist would attribute some of his less endearing traits to this early, forcible rejection by his mother. It wasn't the sort of episode that would produce a happy, well-adjusted child.

He remembered it this morning as he sat in his aluminium-framed greenhouse, miserably itemising the growing catalogue of his misfortunes. He had with him some old diaries, a photograph album and his book of suicide cuttings, methodically collected over the years as others accumulated Press stories about their heroes.

The diaries were a disappointment, revealing only too painfully how bereft of excitement his life had been. The photographs did little to bolster the idea of a happy and crowded existence, showing him usually in groups, from small boys with bikes to more recent ones taken at the college to which he no longer belonged. In the diaries and the pictures he saw an emotionally-repressed person who was a slave to routine, a person to whom losing had become a habit.

He turned to the suicide cuttings to see how others had effected their escape from this world. There were a variety of options, but you could never tell how swift or painless they had been. He read through each of them in search of enlightenment and inspiration. Some made sure:

After seeing the film, the former lecturer took an overdose of painkillers and tied a plastic bag over her head.

Some seemed to find that it wasn't the straightforward business that they had imagined:

He made repeated suicide attempts over the next five days, slashing his wrists and twice taking overdoses of more than 130 painkillers.

When he failed to gas himself in his Renault, he bought a Talbot Samba in which he was found dead on June 8.

Some were just careless:

A woman and a boy of six were hurt yesterday when a man jumped from a multi-storey car-park bridge into a shopping mall.

Horrified bystanders saw him fall 100 feet to his death in Crawley, West Sussex.

He hit Maureen Wickenden, 46, who later had precautionary X-rays. Her nephew Robbie Massey was treated for a broken arm.

Others did not want to go alone, and at least one was in such a hurry that he didn't care who he took with him:

Investigators in Morocco say the crash of an airliner near Agadir on Sunday was caused by the pilot's decision to commit suicide.

All 44 people on board were killed in the crash.

The Transport Ministry said the pilot switched off the automatic navigation equipment and directed the plane towards the ground.

195

The Royal Air Maroc ATR-42 turboprop crashed in the Atlas Mountains.

Jones had often joked in his humourless way of drowning himself in a vat of banana daiquiri, but his inclination had always been towards hanging, and he was surprised at how few people in the cuttings had arrived at that final choice. He realised that he had already made it himself because he had come out to the greenhouse to find the rope. He picked it up, ten yards of it, the 'hemp necktie' of the old lynch mobs, he told himself, and put it on his lap.

Although it had never seemed imminent, he had always felt that suicide would be the way that he would go, and years of considering the prospect had produced, now that the moment had arrived, a remarkable calm.

He felt the rough texture of the rope and wondered what to do with it. Despite a lifelong obsession and copious research, the intricacies of death by hanging were still not entirely clear to him. The body-weight and the knot under the chin to snap the neck constituted technical information that he wasn't equipped to absorb; it was alien to his area. And yet, he told himself reproachfully as he fingered the rope, in British remand centres up and down the country teenagers were hanging themselves every week with not much more than a pair of socks.

He realised now that, given his long-term expectations, it had been a mistake to buy a bungalow.

Defenstration, a one-time favourite, had to be removed from his list of choices; hurling yourself from the window of a bungalow wouldn't even sprain your ankle. And more relevantly now, a bungalow lacked the stairs and bannisters from which many a successful suicide had been found hanging.

He needed an energetic launch that would break the neck cleanly and not leave him there dangling and strangling. He picked up his books and took them and the rope into the bungalow to see where best he could do it. He could always jump off a chair or a cupboard if he could find something above him that would hold the rope.

Once indoors he decided on a coffee. His mouth was dry and nerves were beginning to distract him. A soothing dose of caffeine would focus his mind. He put the coffee on the kitchen table and went to look for a reference book that was in this bungalow somewhere and would tell him about knots. In a matter of minutes he had found a whole page of them, with illustrations, and settled down at the table to find one that would suit his purpose. There were more than twenty, some of which he remembered from his brief career as a scout: the fisherman's knot, the stevedore's knot, the surgeon's knot. The reef knot was almost the same as the granny, but neither was of any use to him. He had hoped to find something that looked like a hangman's noose, but this was evidently not a popular knot that the average person would want to make. The nearest was the bowline which produced at its end a serviceable noose, and he sat at the table and tried to make it. It took him a quarter of an hour to thread the rope in the correct way; the fussy design provided plenty of opportunities for mistakes. But finally he had a noose and he put it over his head to check that it would tighten under his chin. It did, and he gave it a little tug to make sure that the knot held, and then loosened it and took it off.

He finished his coffee and got up, astonished at how calmly he was dealing with this. He was so certain now that this was his only option that no doubts or worries arrived to interfere with his planning. He walked round the bungalow, looking for somewhere to tie the rope. He went from room to room — from the dining room to the sitting room, to the bedroom, to the spare bedroom, and to the small third bedroom that Gaynor had commandeered for her sewing machine and her painting and her other little hobbies that he sometimes thought she engaged in only to get away from him. Life's a bitch and then you marry one. He wondered how she was feeling this morning, back with a mother for whom she had seldom had a kind word.

But it wasn't difficult to imagine his mother-in-law's reaction when Gaynor arrived at her front door laden with luggage. Well, she would say, I told you so. The ten-year gap in their ages had worried her from the beginning, and she had dearly hoped that her only daughter would find somebody younger and more dynamic. By this morning, he guessed, there would be a strained atmosphere in the house, as his mother-in-law realised that Gaynor had nowhere else to go.

Well, that problem will soon be resolved, he told himself. She can sell this place, collect the life insurance, and live where the hell she likes.

He wandered from room to room, staring at ceilings that supported nothing but simple light bulbs, hanging there with their chintzy shades. The only thing of any height in any room was the huge wardrobe in their bedroom and it was impossible to see how he could press that into service.

A mild panic overtook him. He had been turning suicide over in his mind for nearly twenty years and now that the time for it had arrived he didn't seem to have the most fundamental requirements.

He went back out into the garden and looked around at his little third of an acre. It was enclosed by natural stone walling and panel fencing. There was the pottery shed and the greenhouse. A brick arch connected the single garage, with its yellow up-and-over door, to the bungalow, and he went to look at that. In many ways it suited his purpose ideally, but it had one disadvantage: it faced the road. Neighbours strolling to the shops would be confronted by the sight of Mr Jones trying to hang himself, and although there were plenty who would not think it necessary to obstruct this event, there were others who would scream and call for help.

He walked round the bungalow and saw suddenly what he must do. The rope must be tied firmly to the chimney and he would jump off the roof at the back of the building where nobody could see him.

Satisfied at last, he went to the garage where his longest ladder lay on the ground along one wall. He picked it up and took it round to the back of the bungalow where he rested it against the roof. He could scramble up there, attach the rope to the chimney and the deed would be done.

He went back into the bungalow for the rope. He paused now, examining himself for some sign of regret, but his single-minded determination had left no room for any such sentiment. He had, he thought, imagined this moment many times, and so he was not the tearful, quivering jelly that most people would be in this situation.

He sat down for a minute to look at his bowline knot, and wondered again whether he should leave a note to somebody. Most people left a message of some sort when they killed themselves but there was nobody he wanted to write to. He no longer felt part of the world they all lived in and was quietly determined to slip away. It was a world in which you were even penalised for enjoying yourself. He had had more fun in the last few weeks than in the previous five years – and where had it got him?

He stood up and took the rope out to the garden and then slowly climbed the ladder and eased himself on to the roof. He looked round to check whether anybody could see him, but even at this height he was obscured from everybody's view. Slowly and with some difficulty he scaled the bungalow's sloping roof. He slipped a few inches once but then held firm. Moving with methodical care he eventually reached the chimney, and took the rope which he had been carrying over one shoulder and began tying an end round the small chimney. He wound it round three times and tied two knots to hold it firm.

He then began lowering himself to the edge of the roof where he kicked the ladder away. It clattered on to the patio.

He put his head in the noose, pulled it tight, and then checked to see how much loose rope there was behind him. There was no more than four feet — it would be taut long before his feet could reach the ground.

Satisfied that everything was in place, he squatted frog-like on the edge of the roof and then, gritting his teeth and closing his eyes, he launched himself into eternity.

'The mystery of men,' sighed Emily Mansfield, sitting in a high-back chair in the Virginia Bottomley Ward at the county hospital. 'What a baffling enigma it is. On the one hand we have Einstein, Tolstoy, Aristotle, Van Gogh, Beethoven, Leonardo da Vinci, Galileo, Voltaire, Shakespeare, Copernicus, Kant and Louis Pasteur. And on the other we have—'

'Vernon Jones,' croaked Oscar Mansfield, who was lying on his back in bed with a bandaged head. His leg, encased in plaster, was suspended by a pulley over his head, and there were more bandages on both wrists.

'And on the other we have the rest,' said Emily Mansfield, who had never relished interruptions. 'Men with an unfathomable ability to do something bloody stupid if sex or money are involved. I don't care whether it's a cabinet-maker or a Cabinet Minister. That great brain thumping away in there, and they're led to perdition by their balls or their wallet.'

She sipped a cup of lukewarm tea that a Jamaican nurse had brought her and looked at her battered husband.

'Take Vernon Jones,' she conceded. 'Enjoying himself with a young student regardless of the consequences that he must have known would catch up with him. He had a perfectly respectable job, a good home, a nice wife. Look at Julian Wyatt, killing himself with worry because greed drove him to borrow money and start up a firm in a recession. Colin Dunbar is just as crazy, buying a bar that was not a good business prospect just because he liked bars. And you, my love,' she said, pointing with her teaspoon at her damaged husband, 'the fat spider at the centre of this web of greed, *you* concoct a daft scheme that has men hoping their friends will die. The consequences so far are that Julian has left his wife, Gavin won't have a father, Jones has lost his wife and will soon lose his house, and you're in hospital with some people no doubt hoping that you never come out. None of these things would have happened if it was women we were talking about. The mystery of men! How can they be so clever and on the other hand be the most stupid, feckless creatures on earth?'

'Testosterone,' said Oscar Mansfield.

'What?'

'A potent steroid hormone, the driving force that gives men ideas.'

'Balls,' said Emily Mansfield.

'Those too,' said Oscar. 'Can you pass my tea?'

Emily Mansfield got up and held the cup while Oscar drank. 'You can't confront it, can you? You don't recognise your own folly. Your friends' own folly. Anyway,' she said, 'testosterone didn't seem to do Einstein any harm.'

'He used to sleep for half the day to keep his brain in working order. He didn't have time for the temptations that lure others.'

'How many politicians have been brought down by their sexual antics?'

'I've lost count,' said Oscar Mansfield.

'Exactly. And how many were women?'

'None,' said Oscar.

'Somebody once said that you see loads of bright men with stupid women, but you never see a bright woman with a stupid man. What conclusions do you draw from that?'

'Women are smarter than men?' Oscar tried.

'You're getting there, dear.'

'But you don't have a Voltaire or a Tolstoy.'

'If you weren't a sick man, Oscar, I would hit you.

203

Women have been too busy preparing food, scrubbing floors, laundering clothes and looking after children to enjoy the luxury of sitting down for six uninterrupted hours of thought.'

'I see,' said Oscar. There was an itch on the inside of his plaster that he desperately wanted to scratch. He also, for the first time since the accident, wanted a drink, preferably in the congenial surroundings of the Oasis of Sanity. 'Where's Julian gone, anyway?' he asked.

'I understand that he has moved into Mr Dunbar's establishment,' said Emily. 'It'll make drowning his sorrows that much easier.'

'Julian doesn't drink.'

'I think he'll be drinking by now.'

Oscar had always found it difficult to believe that things really happened when he wasn't there – he imagined the world's population freeze-framed into their respective stereotypes, only coming to life when he arrived on the scene. But now he felt that he was missing something and that events were thoughtlessly unfolding in his absence. The real world, with its dramas and amusements, was somewhere other than this stark room of antiseptic smells and long empty hours.

'When am I going home?' he asked forlornly.

'How are you on crutches?'

'I'll master them if it's going to get me out of here.'

'Is there anything you want?'

'Yes. Get Adrian to mow the lawn.'

'You're thinking about your lawn?' said Emily. 'You must be getting better!'

15

Jones sat on the dustbin, rubbing his elbow.

He must have blacked out, because for a few seconds he couldn't understand why he was there. He looked at the ladder stretched out at his feet which had flattened roses at the edge of the patio, and thought guiltily that he should have put it away. His neck felt sore.

Somewhere a telephone rang relentlessly, but in his daze it didn't sound real: he had that dizzy feeling which was already accompanied by a ringing in the ears. He took a deep breath to clear his head and his mind began operating almost normally. Why was he sitting on a dustbin? was the first question that it raised.

And then it all came back to him and he stood up slowly and looked at the roof. The rope had snapped at the edge, cut perhaps at its contact with the rain gutter. He stood there for a moment feeling confused, and then he walked slowly into the bungalow, needing somewhere to sit down.

The telephone was still ringing and he picked it up unthinkingly. If he had been feeling more alert he would have ignored it.

'Is that Jones?' said a voice when Jones failed to announce himself.

'Jones? Yes,' said Jones, still rubbing his elbow.

'It's Hayes here, Jones. I don't really know how to tell you this.'

'Tell me what?' said Jones, sitting down heavily on a stool. The memories were flooding back now, and he was cursing himself for having picked up the phone.

'I've had a deputation,' Hayes said.

'Deputation?' echoed Jones, trying to place the word. Deputation? Delegation? Degradation? Desperation? Decapitation?

'From the staff,' said Hayes. 'Incredible though it may seem, it turns out that Rosemary Friedland has had sexual intercourse with at least five of them, and maybe seven. At any rate, five of them came to see me and put their cards on the table. In these circumstances I would like to lift your suspension and welcome you back at the college. I can hardly suspend half the staff.'

'Oh, right,' said Jones, who was still struggling to understand.

'Shall we see you tomorrow?'

'Tomorrow?' said Jones. 'Yes, of course.'

He put down the phone and held his head in his hands, trying to shake off a terrible feeling of vagueness. What he really wanted was a long, deep sleep, but just as he was deciding that this was indeed how he would spend the next few hours, there was a knock at the front door.

Again he responded automatically to one of life's little signals and stumbled towards the front door. It was Colin Dunbar who stood smiling on the mat.

'I thought I ought to come and see how you are, Vernon,' he said. 'I don't like to think of my customers marooned in their homes and unable to spend their money in the Oasis because their wives have gone off with their cars, so I just wanted to see whether you need the occasional lift. I'd be quite happy to come down and fetch you.'

'Come in,' said Jones, who found that he was glad of company now.

Colin Dunbar followed him through to the sitting room where they both sat down.

'How did you know that Gaynor had gone?' Jones asked.

'She rang somebody. The gossip gets around. There's so much of it at the moment I can't remember half of it myself. Julian's left his wife on account of your little fling. He now lives at my place — as a paying guest, I'm glad to say. How are you, anyway?'

'Me?' said Jones. 'I'm fine. I've just got my job back, apparently. The girl in question had had half the staff and they've decided that they can't suspend all of them, so I'm reinstated.'

'Wonderful,' said Colin Dunbar, looking round the room. The bungalow, and Jones himself, seemed to be fairly dishevelled. There was mud on the carpet along with an abandoned letter and several unused envelopes. An unwashed cup that had once evidently held black coffee stood neglected on the table with what was obviously a blue movie called *Sunny After Dark*. Jones himself had dirty hands, windblown hair and red dust on his knees and shoes as if he had been crawling over a roof. But there was one thing that Colin Dunbar could hardly ignore, whatever decorum prescribed.

'I hesitate to mention this, Vernon,' he said, with the faintest suggestion of awkwardness, 'but you seem to have some sort of noose round your neck.'

'What? Where? Oh that,' said Jones, feeling a rare flush of embarrassment.

'I haven't interrupted an auto-erotic act, I hope? I've read about constriction of the air supply increasing pleasure.'

Jones smiled wanly. 'The women I'm reputed to have had lately, I don't need that,' he said, removing the noose and dropping it on the floor. 'I was conducting an experiment.'

'An experiment?' said Colin Dunbar. 'Did it work?'

'No,' said Jones. He was feeling a lot better now that he was sitting down indoors and the news from Hayes was beginning to sink in. But he still felt a secret humiliation at his failure. Was he so useless that he couldn't even kill himself? One hundred thousand people attempted it in Britain every year and ninety-five thousand failed. He would have thought, with his morbid devotion to the subject over the years, that he would by now have the expertise to join the triumphant five thousand. People would have reviled his name afterwards for his selfishness and cowardice, but he saw it as a selfless act of great courage.

He asked: 'How's Oscar?'

'Recovering,' said Colin Dunbar. 'His head seems to be working again and the next time we see him he'll be on crutches.'

'So no insurance benefit for you there, then?'

'No,' said Colin Dunbar, thinking how badly he needed £33,000, 'thank God. The Oasis wouldn't be the same without Oscar sitting in the bar.'

'Indeed,' said Jones. 'Well, I think what I'm going to do is refuse your kind offer and hire a car. Then I can go and see Oscar. I owe him an apology, I believe.'

He stood up and began to plan his future.

Julian Wyatt climbed out of bed in the Oasis of Sanity with a jauntiness he had not expected. Birds sang in the trees outside his window, and a bright sun was already climbing into the sky. He had a shower, put on his suit and went down to see what sort of breakfast the Dunbars would provide.

He felt a little like the bachelor he had once been when the only demands that were made on him were made by himself. He got up when he wanted to, went out when he wanted to, ate when he wanted to and ate what he wanted to, watched the television that he wanted to watch and took the holidays that he wanted to take – when he wanted to take them, and not because it was the school holidays. By the time that Fay Dunbar laid a huge fried breakfast in front of him he was beginning to think that, contrary to yesterday's dark thoughts, his life was about to improve in quality.

It wasn't a thought that he could sustain for long, however, as he drove to the office in his Range Rover. The baleful facts about Wyatt Promotions began to infringe upon the optimistic mood that he had almost succeeded in creating. By the time that he had parked his vehicle (driven to work this morning to stop his wife grabbing it) in a shared yard behind the office where a drug dealer did business from the back of a van, he was beginning to wish that he was a thousand miles away.

The technological revolution, which had resulted in screens replacing people, faxes replacing the mail, designers discarding their desks and journalists discarding their pens, had not omitted to penetrate and complicate the straightforward world he worked in. What with online and Internet advertising, train station video-loops and transatlantic inflight videos, he sometimes felt like an old dog who couldn't learn new tricks.

Avis, his secretary, greeted him with the sort of smile that was probably exchanged by inmates of Colditz and, in the current atmosphere of siege, other members of his staff couldn't quite manage to mark his arrival with more than a slight movement of the hand.

He went to his desk and confronted the messages − the demands, excuses, requests and threats − that invariably now occupied most of his morning, and phoned Avis for a coffee.

For the first time he wondered what Lavinia would do this morning. She wasn't the sort of person who would sit around and mope. Already, perhaps, the builder boyfriend had arrived for sexual callisthenics in the conservatory. Or Jones.

He pushed these unpleasant thoughts away and looked at the daily bank statements. As usual, the money was going out in costs and wages rather faster than it was coming in. In this murky world of kickbacks, he realised, he should have been greasing some palms.

Pondering this oversight, he was disturbed by the ringing of the phone which he tucked into his neck so that he still had both hands free to open the unwelcome envelopes.

'Is that Mr Wyatt?' a man asked.

'This is he.' Julian Wyatt did not recognise the voice but knew that the call was important or it would have been fielded by the safe hands of Avis.

'Harris here, Mr Wyatt,' the man said.

Julian Wyatt recalled that he had dealt with a man called Harris recently, but in the prevailing chaos couldn't quite place him.

'Good morning, Mr Harris,' he said. 'Jog my memory.'

'I'm the estate agent you asked to sell your house, Mr Wyatt.'

'Ah, yes. What's the news? Are buyers queueing up for a viewing?'

'Not exactly, Mr Wyatt. The news is not good, I'm afraid.'

The emperor moth can smell a female six miles away, and Julian Wyatt sometimes thought that he possessed a similar aptitude with a crisis. He put down the letters and held the phone in his hand.

'What's the problem, Mr Harris?' he asked.

Mr Harris cleared his throat as if he needed time to find the right words. 'Basically, the problem is your wife, Mr Wyatt. We had a potential buyer before we could even advertise the place, but when we rang your home to arrange a viewing she said the house was not for sale.'

'Not for sale?' Julian Wyatt repeated.

'In fact, she has instructed us to take it off the market.'

'She can't do that, the bitch.'

'She's your wife, Mr Wyatt, and she's living there. We can hardly sell the house over her head. In fact, I see she's listed as joint owner so we need her permission anyway.'

Julian Wyatt didn't say anything and faced with an eerie silence Harris went on talking.

'You'd better get it sorted out, Mr Wyatt. We can't possibly proceed in the present situation.'

'Thank you, Mr Harris,' he said, replacing the phone.

He was sitting at his desk with his head on his chest when Avis came in with the coffee that he had ordered.

'We're ruined,' he said. 'The game's up.'

Oscar Mansfield was lying in his bed, looking with
displeasure at a women's magazine left for him by a
philanthropic hospital visitor. On the cover was a
young model who made her living by staring scornfully
at the public in a thousand well-publicised photographs,
a scorn which Oscar fervently reciprocated.

Jones came in looking sheepish, wearing an old grey
suit. He appeared very tired and had strange graze
marks on his neck.

'Oscar,' he said, extending one hand. 'What can I
say?'

Oscar Mansfield put the magazine down and looked
up. Any visitor was welcome now as each day seemed
longer and emptier than the previous one. His fellow
patients seemed to have been chosen for this ward on
the grounds of their matchless ability to bore the hide
off a rhinoceros, although being kind and feeling far
from scintillating himself, he did wonder whether it
was the ward that had reduced them to the monotonous
and tiresome conversationalists that they now were.

'I suppose "sorry" would seem fairly suitable,' he
said, taking the offered hand. 'Sit down, Vernon. You
look awful.'

'Sorry?' said Jones, sitting down. 'My God, I certainly apologise, Oscar. I've had nightmares thinking about that accident. I don't know how it happened.'

'I think we all know how it happened, given the

way you apparently kept saying "Constanoon, affable" to the copper.'

'Yes, there was that,' said Jones, cringing with shame. '"Afternoon, constable" was difficult to get my tongue round after ten whiskies. How are you, Oscar? What do the doctors say?'

'They say I've got a fracture of the fibula. Three to four weeks in plaster of Paris followed by some intensive physiotherapy. I've got to cut down on the triple toe salchows, double axels and overhead lifts.'

'And what about that bandaged head?'

'I've got medical proof that my brain's all right, which is more than you've got. You can cancel the cruise. I'm on the mend.'

'That's terrific, Oscar,' said Jones, feeling a surge of relief. 'I hope you don't think that those of us who were foolish enough to join your insurance scheme wished you anything but well?'

'Of course not,' said Oscar, smiling. 'What's so foolish about the insurance scheme, anyway?'

Jones shook his head sadly, and embarked on the list of dismal and unforeseen consequences which Oscar had already had to listen to from his wife.

'Even more sinister,' said Jones, 'the day after the accident I had the police round asking if I would profit from your death. If you had been thoughtless enough to pass away, there would have been no world cruise for me. The money would all have vanished in legal fees.'

'The constabulary *are* on the ball,' said Oscar, impressed. 'I'll do a deal with you, Vernon. You smuggle in some nourishment of an alcoholic nature for me, and I'll convince the policeman who came to call on you that the accident was my fault and that I had carelessly failed to notice that you were already in your car and reversing.'

'That would be awfully good of you, Oscar,' said Jones. 'It's been a weight on my mind.'

'Bottles of San Miguel would be acceptable,' said Oscar. 'Don't forget the bottle opener.'

Jones looked at him doubtfully. 'I don't want to get you into any trouble,' he said.

'I don't want to get *you* into any trouble, Vernon. I can see how the police are thinking.'

'Okay,' said Jones. 'San Miguel. I'll get you a crate.'

'It doesn't come in crates. It's in cardboard packs, but you'll have to disguise it.'

'As what?' asked Jones.

'I don't know, Vernon. It's up to you. If they see it's beer they won't let you in. Have you got a car, by the way? Emily told me about your various misfortunes.'

'I've hired a Ford Fiesta. It's much better than my battered old Vauxhall. I've also got my job back.'

'How did you manage that? They put screwing on the curriculum?'

When Jones had told him the story of Hayes's phone call, and the startling statistics of Rosemary Friedland's sex life, Oscar again had the feeling that he was missing too much lying here. He had always hated hospitals and had never had to stay in one.

But he could see that if you had to, the orthopaedic ward was the place to be. In this theatre of terror, the broken bones department was the light entertainment. The terrible things happened elsewhere. In the next ward, apparently, a pretty young girl was dying because one of the mentally disturbed children she was teaching had hit her over the head with a cricket bat. Fear and misery stalked the rundown corridors. Oscar Mansfield knew that it would come to him one day, but not yet. When the neurologist told him gloomily that his head was all right, he resolved to put a little more into his life, and take a little more out. There was no time to waste.

A staff nurse appeared to disperse the visitors who began shuffling with poorly disguised relief towards the exit. Jones lingered, uncertain what to do.

'What's that graze on your neck?' asked Oscar, who was reluctant to see his company leave. 'It looks as if you tried to hang yourself.'

Jones laughed emptily. He had discussed suicide many times with Oscar and felt now the need to talk to somebody about his odd experience on the roof.

'Between you and me, Oscar, I did,' he said. 'I was at the end of my tether. I'd lost my job and my wife and the future was black. It seemed like the right moment to go. It was a dark moment of despair.'

'What happened?'

'The rope snapped.'

'The rope snapped?' said Oscar. 'You mean after all

this learned chat about topping yourself, you didn't even have the right rope?'

'I thought it would be adequate. You can hardly go into a shop and ask, "Is this rope okay for me to hang myself with?" It's not how they grade it.'

'No, I can see that,' said Oscar. 'It's not something that the consumer reports deal with. Still, after all that research and preparation it's a bit of an anti-climax. It's like those air pioneers who crashed on the runway.'

'Sometimes I think you don't take me seriously, Oscar,' said Jones.

'I take you very seriously, Vernon, especially your driving.'

Jones stood up as the nurse came over to ask him to leave.

'San what?' he said.

'Miguel,' said Oscar.

Dear Sir, wrote Emily Mansfield, feeling the need to unleash some irritation and strafe a few sitting ducks. *Is there any job in the world that is so obviously unnecessary as the one held by the collection of eccentrics who try to predict the weather on television? With regional interventions they sometimes appear three times in an hour and what nobody seems to notice is that they are hardly ever right. The more inaccurate they become, the more buoyant they seem, confident no doubt that most people don't remember after a day of remorseless sun that this time yesterday they were telling us to get out our umbrellas. Who believes them? Who pays for them? Who needs them?*

She signed the letter with a flourish, feeling marginally better. Another little critique, about men and their disappointing foibles, was simmering on the back burner, but she wasn't quite ready to serve it.

Instead she decided to go out to post the letter, and then call on Lavinia Wyatt while she had the BMW out.

The deserted wife opened the door in a pink housecoat that stopped at the top of her thighs. She looked some way short of upset.

'Emily, how kind of you to call,' she said, embarrassed. 'How's Oscar?'

'Never mind Oscar,' said Emily, stepping uninvited into the hall. 'I heard about Julian running off and I was worried about you. How are you bearing up? Is there anything I can do?'

Lavinia Wyatt ushered her into the kitchen where the coffee machine was bubbling.

'Julian?' she said. 'Who's Julian?'

'That blond-haired husband of yours with the strained expression.'

'Oh, *that* Julian. I have to be honest, Emily. So far his departure has hardly been noticed. Coffee?'

Emily Mansfield sat down. This was a kitchen that she would have liked herself. It was full of deep pine work surface and pine drawers and cupboards. It had a beamed ceiling.

220

'It's a lovely house,' she said. 'It's a great shame that you've got to sell it.'

When Lavinia Wyatt bent over to place her coffee on the table it was apparent that she was wearing nothing under the housecoat.

'It most certainly is *not* being sold,' she said forcefully. 'I've disabused the estate agent of that idea, and thrown his *For Sale* sign on the next bonfire.'

'Golly, Lavinia,' said Emily admiringly. 'You certainly know how to handle things.'

'If Julian wants to leave me, that's up to him. But he needn't think he's going to sell my house. I live here. I like it. He'll have to continue paying the mortgage and find somewhere else for himself.'

'Well,' said Emily, 'I came here thinking that I might be able to help you in some way, but you don't seem to need it.'

She was suddenly aware of a man standing in the doorway. He was a young, rather handsome man who was naked except for a pink towel round his waist. His body was exceptionally muscular and deeply tanned.

'Come on, bird,' he said. 'I've got to be on site at twelve.'

Emily Mansfield finished her coffee quickly and stood up.

'I've got to be off, too,' she said.

16

In the despairing hope that catastrophe could yet be averted, Julian Wyatt invited Hendon to lunch at a fashionable restaurant where the décor seemed to be based on a set from a Diaghilev ballet. It turned out that the place was indeed Russian and had twenty-one different vodkas to prove it. Julian Wyatt, summoning up reserves of sanguineness that were no longer suited to his situation, hoped that such unprecedented generosity would produce a less hostile reaction than the one that would certainly greet him in Hendon's office.

The bank manager selected a herb and spiced vodka, flavoured with bison grass. He proved to be an omnivorous eater.

'What's the news then, Julian?' he asked, using first names here that he would never resort to in his office. 'Is it boom time at Wyatt Promotions?'

'Boom time is pushing it,' said Julian Wyatt, marvelling at his capacity for understatement. 'The firm ticks over, but I have a problem.'

'Of course,' said Hendon. 'That's why you invited me to lunch.'

Julian Wyatt dabbled unhappily with his chicken Kiev. He could think of no way in which he could dress up what he had to say to make it more palatable.

'My wife has been unfaithful to me,' he announced very formally.

Hendon paused only briefly in his assault on his food, a lamb kebab which had followed blinis, caviar and cured salmon. 'I'm sorry to hear that,' he said. 'However, is this a problem for your bank manager?'

'I'm afraid it is,' said Julian Wyatt. 'You see, I've left her. I no longer live at home.'

'The nuclear family has gone into fission,' said Hendon, licking the rim of his glass in a way that made Julian Wyatt feel slightly bilious. 'Divorce, is it?'

Julian Wyatt realised that either he was not leading his listener in the right direction, or Hendon was more obtuse than he suspected. Without the exciting threat of bankruptcy and disaster hovering over him, lunch with Hendon would be about as interesting as a general election in Sweden.

'I haven't got around to considering divorce yet,' he said. 'I've more immediate problems to attend to.'

'I can imagine,' said Hendon, pouring them both vodka. 'I thought you didn't drink?'

'You can't get through my various crises on Perrier water,' said Julian Wyatt. 'By the time this is over I'll need a drying-out clinic.'

'I've got customers who have left three or four

wives,' said Hendon. 'It doesn't seem to do them any harm.'

'Perhaps they didn't begin from the same precarious position as me. You may remember that I planned to sell my house to release some cash and reduce my debt to you?'

'Indeed I do. I was going to ask you how that was going. Has there been much interest?'

Julian Wyatt picked up his vodka and drank quite a lot.

'This is the problem I wanted to discuss with you.'

Hendon stopped eating. 'No buyers in sight? You must bring the price down.'

'My wife is in the house. She refuses to sell. In fact, she's taken it off the market.'

Hendon put down his knife and fork. There could be no clearer indication, thought Julian Wyatt, of how seriously he took this news. He stared at the tablecloth for a while as if trying to recall the exact details of Julian Wyatt's financial predicament.

'I think I made it clear, Mr Wyatt, that the sale of the house was an essential part of the bank's continued support?'

'You did,' said Julian Wyatt sadly. His spirits were not lifted by Hendon's abrupt reversion to his title and surname, nor by the hard look that now inhabited his guest's face. 'I was trying to sell it. I was eager to sell it. But this domestic problem has got in the way.'

'Can't you get it out of the way?'

'I can't think how. Can you?'

'Well, I suppose making it up with your wife would be one answer.'

'I can't do that,' said Julian Wyatt. 'You see, there was more than one man.'

'Christ,' said Hendon, impressed. 'I suppose you've got to admire the energy.'

Julian Wyatt, feeling no compulsion to admire his wife's energy, looked at Hendon with murderous intent. To be at the mercy of this twerp was almost more than he could take. With his inflated self-esteem and his cracked patent leather shoes, he sat there gnawing lamb and making fatuous suggestions while holding Julian Wyatt's fate in his hands. He looked so young but had the gestures and attitudes of a man in his forties, and it was an additional irritation that he spoke in the fashionably classless accent of a young man on the way up, an accent derived from disc jockeys and television reporters, with unexpected emphases and bizarre intonations.

'I've never thought of getting married myself,' he said. 'The UK has the highest divorce rate in Europe, with one in two marriages heading for the courts. The financial implications are horrendous.'

'I thought you had customers who had come through three or four marriages unharmed?'

'Zillionaries,' said Hendon. 'Marriage is a rich man's game.'

He finished his meal and pushed his plate to one side with a thoughtful expression on his face. It emerged that this period of reflection was directed towards his choice of pudding. He stared at the menu, propped upright in the middle of the table, and announced: 'Crème brûlée with fruit in it, I think.'

Julian Wyatt beckoned a waiter and drank more vodka.

'What's going to happen?' he asked.

Hendon looked at him. 'Don't spoil my pudding by asking that. This is some café, isn't it?'

'I hoped you'd like it,' said Julian Wyatt, feeling like a man in the dock awaiting the return of an unfriendly jury. 'It got a good write-up in one of the Sundays. Princess Margaret used to eat here.'

The news of royal patronage brought a complacent smile to Hendon's face, and Julian Wyatt wondered what complexes and insecurities nibbled away behind the façade of assurance and self-belief.

'I must persuade more customers to bring me here,' he said. 'There aren't many perks in my job. No foreign trips, no new car, no private health insurance, no days off on the golf course entertaining clients, no huge expense accounts. I suppose you've got all those?'

Julian Wyatt looked at him expecting to see a glimmer of envy, but encountered instead a look of resentment. It struck him as odd that Hendon, wrapped in the well-paid security of the bank, was trying to depict his life as being in some way less blessed than Julian Wyatt's, who now dangled over the snake pit on a gossamer thread.

'Well, I need to entertain clients, I need an expense

account to take you out to lunch and I need a car,' he said defensively. 'Don't think we're extravagant. We watch every penny.'

'So no port then?' said Hendon.

Julian Wyatt felt caught in a trap, destined to displease this man whichever decision he made.

'Of course,' he said. 'Whatever you want.'

When the plates had been removed and the port had arrived, Julian Wyatt experienced the faintest twinkle of hope. Surely Hendon couldn't eat and drink his way through this expensive feast and then return to the office and pull the plug on Wyatt Promotions? There would be something dishonourable about accepting this hospitality if he planned to destroy his host at the end of it. But then he remembered that when Hendon had sat down at this table he was not aware that Lavinia Wyatt had taken the house off the market. He had been delivered that little bombshell over lunch, and it was obviously this news that he was now turning over in his mind. Julian Wyatt could tell by the frown.

Hendon ran his fingers through his thick black hair and the frown mutated to a scowl. 'I'll have to refer this upwards,' he said. 'It's a new situation.'

'Upwards?'

'Regional Office. Head Office. I don't know.'

'Can't you make a decision?' asked Julian Wyatt, believing without even the flimsiest justification that Hendon's verdict would be more sympathetic than that of an unknown banker in the City.

'Out of my league, I'm afraid,' Hendon said. 'We're

talking about a lot of money here, and we've left the equity behind.'

Julian Wyatt didn't like the sound of any of this. 'Can't you at least make a recommendation, based on your knowledge of Wyatt Promotions?'

Hendon's glumness deepened. 'The truth is I'm probably going to get a rocket for going in so far. I doubt whether they'll listen to me at this stage.' He picked up the port and finished it with a gulp. 'Obviously I'll say what I can — to defend my position as much as yours, quite frankly. But it's not good. You've changed the rules subsequent to the loan. First you're selling your house, now you're not selling your house. Banks can't operate with that sort of behaviour. It makes them nervous. They don't know where they are. You see the problem?'

Julian Wyatt nodded. He could see nothing but problems.

'I could always murder my wife,' he suggested.

'Okay short-term, bad long-term,' said Hendon. 'Your wife's irrelevant, anyway. It's the house that matters. Couldn't you reach some settlement with her? Send her off with the money to buy a bungalow by the sea?'

'I don't have the money to reach a settlement with her. It's embedded in the bricks and mortar of our home.'

'Ah yes,' said Hendon, doing up one button on his jacket in a signal that he had to go. 'And if you could release the money and gave it to your wife it would destroy the whole point of the exercise.'

'I think you've got it,' said Julian Wyatt.

Hendon stood up. 'That was a wonderful meal,' he said. 'Thank you very much.'

'I hope we have another,' said Julian Wyatt, seeking straws to clutch.

Hendon's wistful expression conveyed beyond misapprehension the improbability of this occasion repeating itself. 'It would be nice to think so,' he said.

On the pavement he waved nervously for a taxi, anxious to be away. When one pulled up he jumped in quickly and departed with a stiff smile.

Julian Wyatt stood on the kerb and examined the bill. By diligent use of the nation's supermarkets, the money mentioned on its bottom line would have fed his family for a week. If I still had a family, he thought.

The vodka hadn't affected him in the way that he expected and he walked back towards his office feeling comparatively clear-headed. A beggar with a long brown beard and a dusty black coat interposed himself before he had walked far and held out both hands as if one would not be sufficient for the largesse about to come his way. He looked thin but young.

'I have no money,' Julian Wyatt told him. 'I'm bankrupt and ruined.'

'Money for a cup of tea,' the beggar said in a Scottish accent.

'You've probably got more than I have,' said

Julian Wyatt, avoiding the man with a neat side-step.

'Bastard,' said the beggar. But as they went their separate ways the jingle of coins came from the beggar's pocket.

Lying in his hospital bed and seething with boredom, Oscar Mansfield considered a piece of information which seemed intrinsically unreliable but had been passed along to him by one of the nurses whose job it was to produce wintry smiles on the faces of the resident invalids. The information was that a man had once climbed Everest on crutches. Oscar Mansfield, who was soon to admit crutches to his life, decided that he didn't believe this or much else. Solitude had made him cynical. There was hardly a cause or an ideal that obtained his grudging assent or support these days, and he judged that under Emily's splendid influence he was moving into a more sceptical phase of his life where everything would be much easier to handle because it would be dismissed with withering scorn at the outset. Politicians, priests, even doctors, would be repudiated as charlatans and fakes, and he would no longer have to bother with their dubious messages.

Feeling that he had quietly shed one of life's perennial burdens, he glanced round the ward and saw Vernon Jones come in through the far door. He was wearing a quilted anorak and carrying a pile of huge books.

Jones, with a face that seemed to tell of a life of

successive disasters, did not look like the conventional hospital visitor, throwing unwanted smiles in all directions, and in normal circumstances would have been about as welcome as a vegetarian in a butcher's shop. But today, with only his confused thoughts to keep him company, Oscar Mansfield perked up at his appearance.

'Vernon!' he said. 'Any fascinating new attempts to top yourself? Razor-blades in a warm bath is edging its way up the charts, I hear.'

Jones placed eight big books on the chair beside Oscar's bed and straightened up with relief. 'How are you, Oscar?' he asked. 'How's the leg?'

'Getting better every day. What have you brought me? Books? I'm not a bibliophile, Vernon.'

'No, you're bibulous. Open them.'

Oscar picked up the first one, an enormous encyclopedia of compelling facts, and read aloud: 'The longest sausage in the world was thirteen miles long. How interesting. A nanosecond is a billionth of a second. Do I need to know this?'

'Open it some more,' said Jones.

Oscar Mansfield turned more pages and discovered that the centre of the book had been cut out to provide the hiding place for a bottle of San Miguel.

'Here's the bottle opener,' said Jones, putting it on the bed.

'How ingenious,' said Oscar, picking up the second book. 'Do you think you should have done this with Krafft-Ebing's *Psychopathio Sexualis*? I seem to have heard that it's full of fascinating filth.'

'Those bottles are nine inches tall,' said Jones. 'They need big books.'

'Were you once a spy, Vernon?' Oscar asked, slipping a bottle of beer beneath his sheets. 'Did you dabble in espionage?'

'I saw a film once,' said Jones. 'Don't drink too much or I won't have a library left.'

'Don't let's have any comparative judgements between a bottle of San Miguel and a novel by Jeffrey Archer, Vernon. I might think the less of you. What's going on out there in the big wide world?'

Jones sat on the edge of the bed as the chair was now covered with books. 'I went back to work today.'

'Tremendous,' said Oscar. 'And did you get your leg over?'

Jones's return to the college had been greeted with some embarrassment by those teachers who had felt obliged to confess to the Head about their enjoyable physical experiences with Rosemary Friendland, many of them having previously supposed that they were the girl's only lover. The discovery that they were only unregarded members of a troupe, seduced, emptied and discarded with dispassionate efficiency, had demolished their extrovert personalities, and they gathered in the staffroom like victims of a siege.

'Where is she?' Jones had asked.

'As far away as possible,' said Chandler with a shudder. Chandler was a small bald-headed man who operated in one of the science laboratories, and it was difficult for the others to imagine any woman wanting to make love with him, let alone one with the bounteous attributes of Rosemary Friedland.

'She's been shown the door,' said Davidson, the Head of French. 'Her life is downhill from now on, I suspect. Hayes told her that no member of the staff was safe with her in the college. I understand she's gone to London, where her talents will no doubt be appreciated.'

'I appreciated them,' said Jones sadly. 'I thought she was wonderful.'

'Well, now we've put our necks on the block to get you back on board, I hope you'll stick to tutoring,' said Chandler.

'Yes, thank you, gentlemen,' said Jones, recalling disconsolately the fresh smell of the cornfield. 'Your brave support saved my life.'

In the classroom the students accorded him a hero's welcome, surprised and delighted to discover in one so stuffy the predilections and capabilities that they admired most. The Students' Union had produced some distasteful and prurient banners on sticks, the more acceptable of which said CO-JONES IS OUR MAN! and WELCOME BACK, BONKER. Jones banished the banners and resigned himself to his new nickname.

When he had left Oscar Mansfield with his secret hoard in the hospital, he climbed into his hired Fiesta and drove to the Oasis of Sanity. The windswept clouds that had prompted him to don his anorak had been replaced by a warm sun, and the change in the weather and the dramatic reconstruction of his life put him into an uncharacteristically good humour.

He walked into the bar whistling, and found Julian Wyatt with his head on the counter as if he were asleep. Beyond him stood Colin Dunbar, looking as if he had just witnessed a particularly bloody road accident. By way of explanation, he pointed at Julian Wyatt and shook his head, an explanation that explained nothing to Jones who asked: 'What's wrong?'

At the sound of his voice, Julian Wyatt shot up as if he had been hit. 'The architect of my misfortune,' he said, peering drunkenly at the new arrival. 'I owe my downfall to this man.'

'I think that's a bit strong, Julian,' said Colin Dunbar, quickly assuming the role of peacemaker. 'It's more complicated than that.'

Jones, reluctant to jettison the sunny mood he had brought in with him, said: 'A pint of lager, Colin.' After what he had been through in the last week, the hostility of Julian Wyatt was a trifling affair. 'What seems to be the matter?' he asked, as Colin poured his pint.

'*Seems* to be?' said Julian Wyatt. '*Seems* to be? There's nothing illusory about it. I'm facing harsh realities here.'

'Julian's firm's gone down,' said Colin Dunbar. 'The bank withdrew support this afternoon.'

'I'm sorry to hear that,' said Jones. 'I really am.'

Julian Wyatt turned to him and jabbed a finger

235

at his chest. 'I'm going to be made bankrupt. I've lost my family, I've lost my house, and I've lost my money. What do you think of that, Jones?'

'I think it's bloody sad, Julian, but don't lay the blame at my door,' he said. 'Have a word with Lavinia. She came round with the express purpose of having sex with me. There were knickers on the floor before I could shut the front door. She thought I had a heart complaint and that sex would kill me. She thought you'd get the £33,000. Your wonderful missus, Julian, came round to murder me.'

'The no-good bitch,' said Julian Wyatt, pushing an empty glass into Colin Dunbar's waiting hand.

'You might as well blame Oscar for his insurance idea,' said Colin. 'That's where it all starts, kid.'

'The bastard,' said Julian Wyatt. 'Let's go round and break his other leg.'

It was apparent now to Jones that Julian Wyatt had been dealing with his misfortune in a time-honoured way: immoderate quantities of alcohol had vanished down his throat and he viewed the world now through a hopeless haze.

'It wasn't even me that did any wrong,' he said. 'But I'm the one who's going to suffer.'

The others considered this, feeling that Julian Wyatt must have done something wrong to have placed himself in this mess, but he seemed too upset and confused to listen to candid judgements. Instead, he pulled a chequebook and a gold pen from his pocket.

'I must owe you something for my room,' he said to Colin Dunbar. 'Let's pay you while I can.'

Colin Dunbar looked at the cheque before putting it in the till. 'This piece of paper was probably worth more before you scribbled over it,' he said.

'You're right,' said Julian Wyatt. 'Give it back. I'll pay you with a credit card.'

When this transaction had been completed, Julian Wyatt relapsed into a morose silence. He thought about his father who bought Poseidon shares at fourpence ha'penny and sold them for eighteenpence, not knowing that they would soon be worth £100 each. His father was dead now, from no recognisable cause. Julian Wyatt thought that, like an animal, he had lost the will to live and Nature did the rest. There were some families who made money whichever way they turned. The gift was passed on from father to son, like a large nose or alopecia, and the fortune swelled without appreciable effort. The Wyatt family was clearly not in this category, having instead an apparently inherited capacity to turn gold into dust.

'The sum total of Oscar's scheme so far seems to be two broken marriages and a bankrupt business,' said Colin Dunbar, pouring himself a drink. 'I wonder what other little delights it will produce? I suppose you're going to lose your bungalow in the domestic upheaval, Vernon?'

Jones regarded this possibility without concern. The disappearance of his wife had not, so far as he could see, adversely affected his life in the way that he imagined when she walked out. In fact, he felt more relaxed and free than he had for years. Getting his job back had lifted the terminal despair which had afflicted him only yesterday, and losing the bungalow would probably be beneficial too. It did not have happy memories, particularly with a piece of rope still hanging from the chimney.

'I'll get a little flat,' he said. 'I never liked gardening.'

'Have you heard from Gaynor?' Colin Dunbar asked.

'No, but my mother-in-law rang to ask what the hell was going on. Apparently Gaynor couldn't quite bring herself to tell her mother about the girl in the cornfield, so she was left mystified by the whole business.'

'What did you tell her?'

'Basically, that I'd taken up shagging,' he announced to explosions of mirth. 'You can't be elliptical with my mother-in-law or the truth you're trying to convey goes winging past her like a missed penalty. I must say she took it very well. I almost got the impression that I'd gone up in her estimation and, given half a chance, she'd be along for a quick jump herself.'

'And given your form, you wouldn't have turned her down,' said Julian Wyatt. 'From whence does this sexual energy derive, Jones? I always had you down as an impotent old pedant. Now people are locking up their daughters.'

Jones attempted a modest smile. The role of Lothario had arrived late and unexpectedly, but he enjoyed it a lot more than the crumbly image that he had carried around for years. Now that Gaynor had gone, it was a role that he could develop and exploit. Obviously Rosemary Friedland and Lavinia Wyatt were no longer available, but there were other women, other girls.

'I haven't worn myself out by devoting my life to the pursuit of wealth,' he told Julian Wyatt. 'I keep in touch with culture and history. I work short hours and take long holidays, and don't damage my health by rendering myself insensible with drink at every opportunity. The life-force is unharmed.'

'And now no woman is safe. Jones the Stud.'

'They call me Bonker at college,' said Jones, with the transparently bogus modesty that might have accompanied news of a forthcoming appearance in the Queen's honours list.

'Christ,' said Julian Wyatt. 'Give me another drink.'

'Of course,' said Jones, 'by the time that my wife has finished an expensive chat with her solicitor I shall be comprehensively buggered, but it seems to me that nobody round here can face the future with an overdose of optimism.'

'Talking about overdoses,' said Julian Wyatt, 'you used to be the resident suicide consultant in here. Which is the one you recommend? Give us a clue.'

'It depends on your metabolism,' Jones told him. 'Some people take a huge overdose and survive, others take small ones and die. I should stick to whisky.'

'What I really need,' said Julian Wyatt, 'is one of

my fellow trustees to do the decent thing and quietly expire before I'm too poor to pay the premiums. Can't one of you bastards drop dead? I need someone to make a selfless gesture round here.'

He knocked back his whisky and looked up at the others, but volunteers did not rush forward.

17

Fay Dunbar, up early as always to get her daughter off to school and now to cook breakfast for the lone guest upstairs, was developing the feeling of imprisonment that a woman can get when she suddenly realises the restrictions that have been placed on her by having a family. Her life was slipping past and she was spending it in a kitchen. She yearned for a glimpse of the safari parks of Africa, the Australian outback or even the cloudy lakes of Switzerland.

The Oasis of Sanity managed, without attracting the hungry hordes they had hoped for, to consume most of her time. When she wasn't cooking, she was cleaning, or buying, or filling the washing machine and then ironing clothes, tablecloths and towels. There were only occasional bright moments. 'Put one in front of the bill,' a customer had said the previous evening. 'My boss would never believe I've eaten so cheaply.'

On this morning, as her wilful daughter Hannah showed a perceptible reluctance to leave her Cindy dolls for the more rigorous demands of the classroom, she greeted her late-rising husband with the sort of expression that took the shine off his day before it had begun.

'Find out what Julian wants for breakfast,' she said, brushing her daughter's hair.

'David Worsley-Tonks wrote me a letter,' said Hannah. 'I think he loves me.'

'Don't marry him,' said Fay. 'You'll end up in a kitchen.'

'I'll be surprised if Julian wants any breakfast,' said Colin Dunbar, who had a hangover himself. 'After what he drank last night I doubt he can climb out of bed.'

But when he went out of the kitchen he found Julian Wyatt sitting white-faced in the small restaurant area, reading the *Daily Telegraph* and waiting for food.

'The first day of the rest of your life,' said Colin Dunbar. 'Welcome to a world without work.'

Julian Wyatt put down his paper. 'An idea protruded through the alcoholic haze last night, Colin. I thought I could be of some use to you. I'm not a man to sit on his backside doing nothing. It occurred to me that if I were to run the bar, you could do the cooking and give Fay a night off. She looks as if she needs it.'

'It's a brilliant idea, but can you run a bar?'

'Been studying it for years.'

'I'll tell Fay, who wants to know your breakfast order, incidentally.'

'Scrambled eggs, bacon, toast. A few pints of tea and a kind word.'

'You can take the day off,' Colin Dunbar told his wife in the kitchen. 'I'll drive Hannah to school and you can shoot off to Harvey Nicks.'

'How can I do that?' Fay asked.

'Mr Wyatt is deputising for me, and I'm deputising for you.'

'Terrific,' beamed Fay. 'I'll ring Emily Mansfield. She's always saying that she likes to go to London every so often. A day off? You don't have to ask me twice.'

By the time that Colin Dunbar returned from delivering his daughter to the small school where she seemed to be learning more about boys than any of the subjects on the curriculum, his wife had gone and Julian Wyatt was leaving the building in his grey tracksuit.

'I may be poor, but I'm going to be fit,' he said. 'You'll probably get some unpleasant phone calls for me from people called accountants. Tell them I've emigrated.'

'I never talk to accountants on principle,' said Colin Dunbar. 'They scramble my brains.'

Julian Wyatt jogged off down the lane at a pace which Colin Dunbar found painful to watch, but he had to admire the way in which Julian seemed to be putting the bad news of yesterday behind him. He went indoors to sweep the bar, and prepare his establishment for the voracious and gluttonous hordes who never appeared. Mid-morning he made himself a coffee and sat down with Julian Wyatt's newspaper. When aching doubts glided into his mind about the wisdom or otherwise that he had shown in buying the Oasis of Sanity, he consoled himself with the chastening thought that he couldn't do much else. No outstanding talents had revealed themselves during his education at a boys' school just outside London, and the Careers' Master whose job it was to direct departing pupils into congenial slots where they would do least harm, found in Colin Dunbar a strong and amiable youth who refused to be categorised.

A few years earlier, the pupils were all going into the civil service, and a few years later into the City, where they shouted their way to extraordinary salaries, dealing in commodities of one sort or another. But when Colin Dunbar's education had run its erratic course, everybody was going into computers and, having no better idea, he went too. As the years passed and the economy, artificially boosted but authentically deflated, began to falter, Colin Dunbar and the people he worked with believed that something as up-to-the-minute as computers would be recession-proof. When this proved not to be the case, and his firm embarked on something which they humourlessly described as a 'headcount reduction programme', he spent an unhappy three months looking for somebody who would hire him at a time when nobody was seeking to enlarge their staff; so instead he decided to hire himself. From deciding to be self-employed, to buying the Oasis of Sanity, was a very short step for a man with no outstanding talents, but sometimes today he wondered whether it wouldn't have been better if he had left Fay to manage her secretarial agency where the money was both good and regular, rather than consign her to the kitchen where it was distressingly intermittent.

Money was the current preoccupation, too, of Julian Wyatt as he loped down leafy lanes and found that he could obviate the pain of running by filling his mind with something else. But the subject that offered itself for consideration was no less painful, and soon he was imagining the dire events that must be taking place now in his office where yesterday tears had replaced the laughter. The tears came from the girls who were cruelly shaken by news that had come as no surprise to the men. What had surprised the men was that Wyatt Promotions had lasted so long. The only positive reaction to the bank's decision had come from one of the design artists who suggested that a concerted raid on the drinks cabinet would be not only appropriate but also essential as the stuff would only fall into the hands of the liquidator in the morning when he came to appropriate the assets. The injustice of this prospect created huge thirsts and by the time that Julian Wyatt made a sad little speech and then left early, unable to bear it any more, people were falling into broom cupboards and waste-paper baskets as if it was the office party on Christmas Eve. By this morning, some of them would no doubt be feeling as sad and worried as himself, he thought as he ran along the bottom of a sloping field. Some had families with two or three children, most had mortgages or debts of some kind. Only a few could face the future confident of a job offer.

What hurt most, he decided as he embarked on his

third mile, was his conviction that with the bank's support the firm could have survived. The long-term prospects were good: he had a busy team, and business came in, even if it needed borrowed money to fund it. It was the debts that he'd brought with him when he first started up – debts with fluctuating interest rates, that continually postponed the elusive milestone of outright profit.

Half an hour's running brought him to Gerry's Gym, and he went in, more for the conversation than for the torment of further exercise. Three or four attractive ladies were tenaciously pursuing the goal of physical perfection on various machines while Gerry's devoted gaze testified to the success of their efforts.

'Stop staring at the girl on the chest exerciser, Gerry,' Julian said, when his breathing permitted speech.

'I wasn't staring,' said Gerry. 'I was resting my eyes on her. What are you doing in here at this time of day?'

'I'm in a negative employment situation,' said Julian Wyatt, sitting down. 'My life is in ruins.'

'You look ever so slightly stressed,' said Gerry, who looked as fit as ever. 'Firm gone bust?'

'The firm's gone bust, I've left my wife and quite soon I won't have any money.'

'Apart from that, how are things?' said Gerry. 'You're in a classic stress situation, and you don't look as fit as my customers are supposed to look.'

'I've felt better,' admitted Julian Wyatt.

'When you've relaxed for half an hour I'll take

your blood pressure. Your lifestyle was never healthy.
What's your sex-life like?'

'What's a sex-life?'

Gerry gazed at the woman on the chest exerciser and
smiled proudly. 'She was quite flat-chested when she
came to me,' he murmured. Julian Wyatt watched the
energy being so enthusiastically squandered all round
him and wondered how he had ever had the strength
and vitality to spend his off-duty hours in a gym. The
peaks of fitness and robust health towards which
his efforts were supposed to have directed him had
evaporated like morning mist, and today he felt weak
and debilitated and in need of rest.

After half an hour Gerry went to his office and
returned with an Omron digital blood-pressure monitor
which he placed on Julian Wyatt's left forefinger.

'Mental worry can raise your blood pressure,' he said.
'You look like a classic case of hypertension to me.'

'I thought you put a bag thing round the arm?' Julian
Wyatt said.

'Things have moved on since then,' said Gerry.
'Blood pressure on the finger is just as good a test
and a hell of a lot easier. Now let's have a look.
You should be about one hundred and twenty over
seventy.'

'What does that mean?'

'The first number is the systolic pressure when the
heart is pumping out blood. The second is the diastolic
pressure when the heart dilates. Keep still. I've had
people in here wanting to join the gym, I've taken their

247

blood pressure and sent them to their doctors instead. One bloke was in hospital the same day. I have to be careful. People dropping dead in my gym would be bad for the image.'

'What causes hypertension?' asked Julian Wyatt, looking at the little gadget that was now locked on his finger.

'Stress, fatigue, smoking, excessive eating or drinking. Excessive intake of salt. Jesus! Look at your figures!'

'What are they?'

'One hundred and seventy over one hundred and twenty. That's not good, Julian.'

'How bad is it?'

'Well, I should see your doctor, for a start. He'll give you something. And you'd better cut out the jogging until those figures come down. You're obviously under more pressure than I thought.'

'I've lost my firm, Gerry,' said Julian Wyatt, by way of explanation as the finger monitor was removed.

'Well, now you can learn to relax. It could be the saving of you.'

'I need money,' said Julian Wyatt, 'to buy food.'

'I haven't seen anybody starving in the street for ages.'

'My marriage is over.'

'Another cause of stress removed from your life.'

'You make it sound as if I've had a result.'

'We learn to think positively at Gerry's Gym. The mental approach is every bit as important as the

248

physical. We never overlook the mental condition because the brain affects the body.'

Julian Wyatt stood up. 'Thanks for the lecture. Have you any idea how I'm going to get back to the Oasis of Sanity?'

'I think I'd better give you a lift in my car,' said Gerry.

Emily Mansfield parked the B.M.W. in the underground car park in Cadogan Place, her starting-off point for many another assault on the capital's glitziest stores. Unlike most other women, her interest was not in the cream sweaters and silk taffeta puffball skirts that Fay Dunbar had expressed an interest in, nor any of the other overpriced clothes that were displayed enticingly in the places they would visit. Emily Mansfield's tastes ran to the utilitarian, to the mug racks, the apple peelers, the ceramic rolling pins, the asparagus steamers and the garlic bakers that would enhance her kitchen. But first, with their destination achieved, there was coffee.

'I sometimes get the feeling that we are an endangered species,' she said when they were sitting down in the restaurant in Harvey Nichols.

'We?' said Fay Dunbar. 'Who's we?' This unexpected escape from the ceaseless demands of the Oasis of Sanity had produced an exuberant mood she had not known for months.

'The wives,' said Emily Mansfield. 'You may have noticed that there used to be four of us. Now there are two — us.'

249

'I see what you mean,' said Fay Dunbar, dropping a non-fattening sweetener in her coffee. 'Well, Lavinia was always a tart, wasn't she? And it's her fault that Gaynor left.'

'I'm glad you see it that way. Myself, I'm more inclined to blame my old man.'

'Poor Oscar,' said Fay Dunbar. 'I don't see how we can blame him for two broken marriages.'

'There's a causal link between his wonderful insurance idea and most of the disasters that followed. The link is this: if there hadn't been an insurance project, there wouldn't have been any disasters.'

'Poor Oscar wasn't to know,' said Fay Dunbar. 'Don't blame him for the morals of Mrs Wyatt. He thought he'd come up with a nice idea. Colin was delighted to join.'

'I bet he was, being the youngest,' said Emily Mansfield. 'He could end up with a home in the sun.'

'With his family,' said Fay Dunbar.

'I hope so, but where men are concerned there are few certainties. Look at Jones. Hardly a candidate for unbridled lust, I'd have thought. The earth turns once and he's jumping on anything that moves.'

'Emily, you're so cynical,' said Fay Dunbar, laughing. 'Vernon Jones isn't typical of anything.'

'Vernon Jones is a man, Fay, and therefore heir to a multitude of psychological defects, mental failings and physical weaknesses. They don't have the healthy, single-minded application of women. That's why Mrs

Thatcher was so successful. It takes very, very little to
divert them.'

Emily Mansfield put down her coffee, pleased with
this early test-run of a letter she would write one day.
Fay Dunbar's reaction was less effusive than she might
have hoped, but Fay was young and still untainted by
life's disappointments that usually flourished when men
were around.

'Do you have to hurry back this evening?' she
asked Fay.

'Certainly not. I've been given the whole day off.'

'Let's go to the theatre then,' said Emily Mansfield.
'We might as well make a day of it.'

'What a good idea.' Fay was delighted. 'Let's go to
one of Andrew Lloyd Webber's musicals.'

'Andrew Lloyd Webber,' mused Emily Mansfield.
'How many wives has he had so far?'

As Colin Dunbar had seldom cooked, and Julian Wyatt
had never worked behind a bar, the unruly spirit of
a boys' party prevailed in the Oasis of Sanity that
evening as each declined to take his unfamiliar duties
too seriously. It was an evening that was scheduled to
be quiet, even by the place's slack standards, and the
two men had no higher ambition than to get through
the session peacefully and to enjoy themselves.

'It will be a limited menu tonight,' Colin Dunbar
said. 'I can only do two things with a potato, boil it
or turn it into chips.' The chip-fryer, filled with fat,
was already warming up.

Julian Wyatt was trying to familiarise himself with the locations of the various bottles. He had intended to drop in on his doctor for a chat about his blood pressure, but when he got back from Gerry's Gym he discovered that the liquidator had already arrived and taken away the Range Rover which was listed as an asset of Wyatt Promotions. This deprivation was no more than he had expected, and he resigned himself with no great feelings of regret to the fact that he was now confined to the Oasis of Sanity.

'We'd better start with a drink,' he said.

A couple came in for steak and chips, a young man and a girl who had arrived on a bike — the same bike, Julian Wyatt saw, when he glanced out of the window at a gleaming blue tandem propped against a tree. Colin Dunbar retired to the kitchen to cook, but took his drink with him. The couple wanted Coca-Cola while they waited for their food. Julian Wyatt wasn't convinced that Coca-Cola-drinking cyclists would add to the gaiety of the evening.

Two men arrived in a car and ordered pints of bitter, but then retired to a corner of the room where there was a table and they could lay out and discuss some architect's drawings.

Jones came in looking appreciably cheerier than usual, ordered a pint of lager and announced that Gaynor had gone to live in Minehead where she had discovered the Lord Jesus.

'I didn't know He lived in Somerset,' said Julian Wyatt.

'Lots of stables in Somerset,' said Jones. 'Sort of thing He's used to.'

'How did this news reach you? Bolt of lightning?'

'My mother-in-law rang again. We get on quite well now I don't live with her daughter.'

A man and his wife came in just after that. He wanted whisky and she wanted a gin and orange.

'It's a long time since I heard anyone ask for a gin and orange,' said Julian Wyatt.

'It's a long time since I've been out,' said the woman sullenly, as if her taste was being called into question. 'Can we see a menu?'

'I hope their cooking is better than their spelling,' said the man, looking at it.

Julian Wyatt pulled himself another pint and dropped the money in the till. Already he had more customers than he wanted, but now he had one more. A sun-tanned young man in jeans and a white vest came in and sauntered up to the bar. Julian Wyatt wanted to tell him that he fell short of the sartorial standards demanded in the Oasis of Sanity, but he wasn't sure it had any.

'Seen your picture,' said the man when he reached the counter. 'You're Julian.'

'You're telling me something I already know,' Julian Wyatt said. 'Can I get you something?' His lack of enthusiasm for this man was tranquillised somewhat by the customer's extraordinary muscular development and the flinty look in his unintelligent brown eyes.

'Your missus sent me,' the man said, placing two

large hands on the edge of the counter. 'She's not happy.'

Julian Wyatt tried to disguise the fact that this news, so far from being an occasion for collective regret, was in truth a disclosure that filled him with feelings of considerable pleasure.

'What's she not happy about?'

'She's had some geezers round from the bank. They're going to sell her house.'

Julian Wyatt had quite forgotten in the general maelstrom that a bank had a charge on the house and that the house, too, would now vanish as swiftly as the Range Rover and Wyatt Promotions itself.

'I can see,' he said, 'how that would piss her off.'

The man in the vest looked at him, not liking the tone of this reply. It was short of the understanding and sympathy that he had come here to find.

'She wants me to tell you that if you don't get this sorted it will end in tears,' he said, leaning closer to Julian Wyatt than was strictly necessary. 'Your tears.'

Julian Wyatt's concern as he stared back at the lean brown face was only for his blood pressure.

'You're the messenger, are you?' he asked. 'I didn't hear your name.'

'Wayne.'

'Yes,' said Julian Wyatt. 'I thought it might be.'

'Lavinia says call off the bank and save yourself a lot of pain.'

'Pain, Wayne?' said Julian Wyatt.

'We're talking broken arms and legs here, Jules.'

This mortifying contraction of his name offended Julian Wyatt more than anything that had gone before. 'Listen, you muscle-bound moron. I don't have to talk to you about my domestic affairs, even if you are the luck-less sod who's screwing my wife. If the cow wants to talk to me, put a halter on her and bring her round.'

The man's reaction to this was surprisingly genial. He smiled broadly, gratified perhaps to have pierced the veneer.

'She doesn't want to talk to you. You're dealing with me, mate,' he said. 'And Lavinia is not leaving the house.'

'Is this man threatening you?' asked Jones, who had felt ignored during this conversation. 'I'll call the police.'

Julian pulled back, conscious of his obligations to the good name of the Oasis of Sanity. Punch-ups and police visits were not the ingredients that helped to popularise a bar.

'Don't worry yourself, Vernon,' he said. 'Mr Wayne and I have finished our discussion.'

Mr Wayne, however, showed no disposition to leave. 'I'll have a pint while I'm here,' he said.

'In that vest?' said Julian Wyatt. 'Go home and get dressed and I'll consider it.'

'Are you refusing to serve me?'

'That sort of thing,' said Julian Wyatt.

The man considered this for a few nobody-pushes-me-around moments, and then decided evidently that his time for revenge would come. 'You'll be hearing from me,' he said, as he walked to the door. 'Count on it.'

'My God,' said Jones. 'I don't admire Lavinia's taste in men.'

'Unnecessarily modest, coming from you,' said Julian Wyatt. 'I hope you won't think me offensive, Vernon, if I say that she doesn't have taste any more. Of course once, in the dim and distant past, she was a discriminating dame, satisfied only to accept the best.'

'And then you rode up on your white horse and the bastions crumbled?'

'That's how it happened,' said Julian Wyatt. 'I should have shot the horse.'

Colin Dunbar now emerged with the steak and chips that the cyclists had ordered, and Julian Wyatt became a waiter, transferring food and cutlery to a table in the restaurant area. The couple who had asked for a menu came up to the counter having decided, after tortured debate, what they wanted to eat.

'What was the matter with the spelling?' Julian Wyatt asked out of interest.

'There's no "e" in tomato,' the man said.

Jones plucked the menu from the man's hand, unable to restrain his pedantic impulses.

'These tomatoes are plural,' he said. 'They have an "e" when they're plural.'

The man looked at Jones as if he had escaped from somewhere and concentrated his attention on Julian Wyatt. 'Chicken and chips twice,' he said. 'With peas.'
The menu they had been shown excluded the more

exotic dishes that Fay Dunbar could prepare, but they seemed to be satisfied with their restricted choice.

Julian took their order into the kitchen. 'What sort of evening are you having, boss?' he asked.

'Hot,' said Colin Dunbar. 'Why are chefs such big, burly bastards? You'd think they'd lose a stone every night in this heat.'

Julian Wyatt was returning to the bar when he was suddenly aware of a bright flash of light behind him and a dreadful cry.

He turned immediately and faced a wall of flames. Beyond them was Colin Dunbar, who was rolling around on the floor and on fire. A blazing chip pan was beside him, the flames from it spreading as burning fat ran across the floor.

'Fire!' he shouted at Jones who could already see it. He tried to remember where he had seen a fire extin-guisher: it was amazing how little you noticed when you sat in the same bar every night. He remembered, though, a pay phone by the door.

Confused and blocked by the flames he turned, but Jones had already snatched a fire extinguisher from the wall and was handing it to him over the counter.

'I'll phone the fire brigade,' he shouted, running across the room.

'And the ambulance,' Julian Wyatt shouted back as he struggled to activate the fire extinguisher.

The flames, smaller now, were licking round his legs. Colin Dunbar's cries had stopped and he was no longer moving about on the floor. In the heat and the smoke and the steam which now filled the kitchen it was difficult to breathe.

The fire extinguisher's obdurate mechanism finally succumbed to his frantic grappling, and he discharged the contents at the inert shape of Colin Dunbar who was immediately engulfed in a wall of steam.

Jones ran in and stared in horror.

'He's not dead, is he?' he asked.

'God knows,' said Julian Wyatt. 'He's badly burned, that's for sure. Fire brigade on the way?'

'And the ambulance.'

They looked at a scene of utter devastation. Everything was charred or black and although the fire was quenched, the subsidiary elements of a fire, the steam and the smoke, still curled into the air while everywhere there was the eerie crackle of scorched kitchen material adjusting itself to cooler temperatures.

'What the hell are we to do?' Julian Wyatt asked. Already his mind had moved ahead to picture how Fay Dunbar would react to this disaster. 'What should we do with him?'

'Put cold water on him,' said Jones. 'It relieves the pain. Where's whatsername — Hannah? Is she upstairs? There could be smoke.'

'Colin took her round to stay with a friend as her mother wasn't here,' said Julian Wyatt, filling a bucket with cold water. He bent down and poured it gently over Colin Dunbar who began to resemble a discarded scarecrow on the morning after a storm. His shirt was black, and his face was red in selective blotches. His eyes were closed.

The fire brigade arrived very quickly. Two men rushed in to check that the fire was out, and what sort of fire it had been.

'Where's the gas?' asked one, heading for corners where smoke still rose.

Two ambulancemen came in soon afterwards.

'The pan caught fire and then he did,' Julian Wyatt explained, leading them to the recumbent figure of Colin Dunbar.

'He's in shock,' said the second ambulanceman, unfurling a stretcher. 'The danger is circulatory failure.'

They lifted him on to the stretcher and headed for the door.

'Where's his family?' asked the first ambulanceman.

'His wife's out for the evening. I'll bring her to the hospital directly she gets home.'

'It looks like third-degree burns. That's very painful. The endings of the sensory nerves are exposed.'

'Will he be okay?' asked Jones.

'He doesn't look good to me,' said the ambulanceman.

They carried their patient out into the night and Julian Wyatt and Jones, having escorted them to the door of the ambulance, went back into the kitchen where the firemen were still checking corners.

'You think a fire's out and then a little blaze starts up from the heat when you're not looking,' said one. 'But I think this one's dead.'

When they had gone Julian Wyatt and Jones returned to the bar and sat down with a drink. The customers had departed in the mayhem, but the diners had left the money for their food.

'I don't see Fay taking another night off,' said Jones.

'Looking at that kitchen I should think it would be some time before she can work again,' said Julian Wyatt.

Fay Dunbar and Emily Mansfield sat in the circle at Her Majesty's Theatre watching *The Phantom of the Opera*. It was the end of a perfect day far removed from the kitchens and the hospitals where they had each lately spent so much time. The shopping had been successful and deeply satisfying, and in the middle of the afternoon they had treated themselves to an extended lunch in one of the best Italian restaurants.

Now they were engrossed in a show that they had both wanted to see. Fay Dunbar stared in fascination at the Phantom in his mask and thought how awful it would be to have a damaged face like that.

18

The following morning when Fay Dunbar drove back to the hospital in the family's Passat, Julian Wyatt went with her, partly to offer whatever comfort and support she needed, but also because he had nothing else to do. After the horror of the previous evening when they had found Colin Dunbar covered in sterile gauze, crêpe bandages and zinc oxide plasters, being fed morphine intravenously and unable to talk, Fay Dunbar this morning was no longer the tense and frightened creature of that first visit. Primed by her conversations with Emily Mansfield, she had settled into a fuming conviction that the blame for this calamity lay with Oscar Mansfield and his crazy ideas.

'If you hadn't joined the insurance scheme, Lavinia wouldn't have gone to see Vernon, you wouldn't have left her, she would have agreed to sell your house to save your firm, you wouldn't have been working in the Oasis and Colin wouldn't have been cooking,' she explained with a furious despair.

Julian Wyatt didn't know how to answer this. A doctor had told him the previous evening that there was a fifty per cent chance that Colin Dunbar would die. He explained in language that Julian Wyatt almost understood that the loss of fluid from the circulating blood at the site of the injuries led to a fall in the volume of circulating blood. The body, attempting to compensate for this loss, withdrew the fluid from the uninjured areas of the body; this, in turn, could damage the liver and the kidneys and result in falling circulation, lack of oxygen and eventually death.

He suggested gently to Fay: 'Not even Oscar could have foreseen that chain of developments. I'm not sure he even knew that my wife is a vindictive and promiscuous slut.'

Colin Dunbar had spent the night in a special resuscitation room until the danger of circulatory collapse had passed.

'You must see him alone first,' said Julian Wyatt. 'I'll join you in a quarter of an hour.'

He sauntered down the hospital's aseptic corridors, remembering suddenly that Oscar Mansfield was closeted here somewhere. His friends were being transferred here one by one, and if the trend continued the centre of his social life would soon be shifted from the Oasis of Sanity to the county hospital. It wasn't an enticing prospect.

Oscar Mansfield, in new red pyjamas, lay despondently in a bed that was covered with books.

'Julian,' he said. 'I understand you've joined me in the ranks of the retired?'

'Involuntarily,' said Julian Wyatt. 'What are all these books?'

'Open one.'

Julian Wyatt picked up a book and opened it. An empty bottle of beer was hidden in its pages.

'There's a full bottle in one of them and I can't find it,' fretted Oscar Mansfield. 'Try that one.'

Julian Wyatt opened three books before he found one that contained a full bottle. Oscar Mansfield took it gratefully and slipped it under his sheets.

'Jones brought me these. Clever, eh? Nice of you to drop in.'

'You're not the only person I've come to see,' Julian Wyatt admitted. 'Something terrible happened last night.'

'Jones try to kill himself?'

'Jones? No. Jones is remarkably cheerful these days. He's kept his job and lost his wife, which is the opposite of what I've done.'

'I thought you'd left Lavinia?'

'But I haven't lost her in the way that Jones has lost Gaynor. She's still about, making demands and issuing threats via her yobbish builder boyfriend.'

'I'm sorry for you, Julian,' said Oscar Mansfield soberly. 'What happened last night?'

Julian Wyatt described the events of the previous evening which he could still hardly believe himself.

'A doctor last night told me he had a fifty-fifty

chance,' he said. 'It wasn't a piece of information I shared with Fay.'

'It's almost as if there's a curse on people in our syndicate,' said Oscar Mansfield. 'First Jones and his problems, then me and the car accident and now Colin. How are you feeling? You don't look that good.'

'I've got blood pressure,' said Julian Wyatt, sitting down. 'Gerry at the gym told me to avoid exercise.'

'Good grief,' said Oscar Mansfield. 'I hope you're up to date on your premiums.'

'The moment is fast approaching when I won't be able to afford them,' Julian Wyatt admitted. 'They're probably going to make me bankrupt.'

'If you're going to default, for God's sake let us know,' said Oscar Mansfield, not anxious to see his grand plan threatened. 'We have a fall-back position in which the others share the cost of your premium until you're back on your feet.'

'Talking of feet, when are you back on yours?'

'I make my debut on crutches tomorrow. Once I've mastered them, they'll let me home.'

Encouraged by this news, Julian Wyatt went to find the other patient. Fay Dunbar was sitting by a bed in which a character from a Frankenstein movie seemed to be swathed in bandages. One eye, almost submerged in bright red flesh, glared malevolently at Julian Wyatt when he entered the room.

'How is he?' he asked.

'Does he take sugar?' asked Colin Dunbar.

'He can talk,' said Fay. 'He's recovering.'

'That's terrific,' said Julian Wyatt, pulling up a chair. 'You had me worried, Colin.'

'About where your next drink was coming from,' said Colin Dunbar. His lips were swollen, one eye was closed, but his brain seemed to be working.

'They're going to do a skin graft on his chest,' said Fay Dunbar. 'And they're feeding him with lovely food — protein supplements with vitamins and iron.'

'Do me a favour, kid,' said the patient. 'Sort out the Oasis, get the insurance man in, then clean the place up and replace what's needed. Get in whatever help you need. Fay'll write the cheques.'

'By the time you come out it will be business as usual,' Julian Wyatt promised. 'In the meantime, we'll keep the bar open.'

'Good man,' said Colin Dunbar, closing his one good eye. 'I think I'll try to sleep.'

The insurance man crept round the charred debris in the kitchen as if he hoped to find conclusive proof of arson. Many of the fires that were expected to separate the insurance company from some of its money had been artfully started by the claimant, and he was adept at exposing this popular little gambit, often producing prison sentences rather than money for his erstwhile customers. But frustration greeted him here. The chip pan had obviously been the centre of the blaze; it was a situation he had seen many times before. He probed in corners of the kitchen in search of the evidence that would save his firm money, even taking photographs of the chaos that surrounded him, but soon admitted defeat and began instead to list the damage and the replacements that would be necessary to restore the kitchen to working order.

'Go ahead and do it,' he said miserably. 'Send us the bill.'

With this *carte blanche*, Julian Wyatt set about clearing up the mess. He spent most of the morning on his hands and knees, and then an hour on the phone talking to firms who could replace the damaged articles. With an alacrity permitted by the inactivity of the recession, they came round in the afternoon, and by six o'clock the kitchen was almost as it had been a day earlier. Only wet paint prevented the resumption of cooking.

'We'll open the bar tonight,' Fay Dunbar decided. 'If anyone wants food I can do sandwiches.'

Julian Wyatt, flushed and hot, fell into a chair. He had engaged in more physical work than Gerry at the gym would have recommended, and his mind still swarmed with the various threats to his mental well-being that were being mounted by Wayne and Lavinia and various hostile gentlemen in London who were now analysing the financial books at Wyatt Promotions and ensuring his downfall. There wasn't anything he could do about any of it, but merely thinking about the events now ensuing that were inimical to his interests made him feel ill.

'I'll take a shower,' he said.

But upstairs in the shower he was afflicted by a dizzy spell and had to stumble out wet to find a seat.

He dismissed it as the consequence of having spent the morning on his hands and knees; he had enough to worry him without an additional concern about his health. He dried himself, got dressed and went down to the bar. Nobody was paying him for all this work, but perhaps the Dunbars would waive his bed and breakfast costs — a small matter which could soon become a serious consideration.

Jones came in first. In a reversal of what had once been the norm, he now seemed to be the most cheerful person around.

'I've bought a little Metro,' he said, once a full pint of lager had been placed within his reach.

'Try not to hit anybody with it,' said Julian Wyatt.

'I've been to see Colin. He's got a large raw area on his chest and they're going to give him a skin graft.'

'How was he?'

'Perking up. He could be out in a week. How are things with you?'

Julian Wyatt sat down behind the counter and picked up his drink. He didn't really want it. 'Do you mean apart from the fact that I've lost my family, I'm going to be made bankrupt, I won't be able to write cheques, I've got nowhere to live and my wife's boyfriend is going to break my legs?'

'Yes,' said Jones, 'apart from that.'

'Well, apart from that I've got amazingly high blood pressure and I don't feel too good.'

'In the days when I considered suicide a serious

option, I don't remember that my life contained misfortunes on that scale,' said Jones enviously. 'It's
awe-inspiring.'

'I'm glad you're impressed. I'll see if I can dig up
fresh tribulations to keep you amused.'

'Out of all of us you were the one that we envied.
The entrepreneur who went out on his own to create an
empire. The lovely house, the lovely wife, the statutory
Range Rover. The bright son at public school.'

'It was an illusion,' said Julian Wyatt. 'I lived on a
knife edge and it's about to cut me to ribbons.'

Jones appeared concerned. 'You can't let it beat you,
Julian. You've got to cheer up. You go round with a
long face and nobody will want to talk to you.'

'We used to talk to you,' said Julian Wyatt. 'When
you stood here discussing the relative merits of jumping
off a bridge or drinking arsenic we used to treat you as if
you were a normal person. You were the most miserable
sod in Christendom and we used to buy you drinks.'

Jones managed to look as if Julian Wyatt's recollec-
tion of this dark period of his life was whimsical exag-
geration, attributable, perhaps, to a memory impaired
by his own multiplying troubles.

'I've had setbacks,' he conceded. 'Things can't go
your own way all the time, but the human spirit, I
find, is an indomitable entity that can survive the most
appalling pressure.'

'There's a farm down the lane with less bullshit than
that,' said Julian Wyatt, 'and several hundred very full
mental homes around to prove you're wrong.'

'But I came through my troubles, Julian,' Jones said earnestly, 'and then things start to look rosier.'

Julian Wyatt couldn't see how his troubles, which were now almost too tangled to unravel, could be replaced by anything rosier than a wreath, but he was prevented from impressing upon Jones the extent of his despair by the unexpected and deeply unwelcome appearance of his wife.

Lavinia Wyatt was wearing a short yellow dress and white shoes. Her suntan suggested that she had spent much of the last few days lying on a sunbed in her garden.

'Good evening, Vernon,' she said, taking a stool at the counter. 'I'm *so* glad you're fit after all.' With the civilities over, she turned on her husband.

'I've had men round,' she said.

'I bet you have,' said Julian Wyatt. 'Who was it — the Parachute Regiment?'

'Abuse isn't going to help here, Julian,' she said with commendable coolness. 'They were men from the receivers or liquidators or whoever they are, and they came to value the house. They said they'll sell it at less than its real value for a quick sale on behalf of the bank. What protection do I have?'

'Wayne?' suggested Julian Wyatt.

'Jesus,' said his wife, looking at Jones. 'Has what he calls his brain finally packed in?'

'You have no protection, Lavinia. You live in a house the bank now own,' said Julian Wyatt.

'They'll have to get a court order to get me out.'

'Yes, and the court will grant it, what with Gavin being at boarding school. The lunatics who run our courts aren't going to decide that you need five bed-rooms, even with your sex-life.'

'Is it possible for you to open your mouth without something offensive coming out?' Lavinia Wyatt asked, brushing an imaginary fleck from her skirt.

A host of offensive remarks about open mouths sprung immediately to Julian Wyatt's brain, mostly to do with his wife's capacity for oral sex, but he was too tired to care.

'What do you want, Lavinia?' he asked wearily.

'That's better,' his wife said, in the manner of an aggravated school-mistress. 'What I want is for you to settle your debt to the bank without my house being involved in the transaction. Find the money somewhere else. Leave me alone.'

'That's a good one,' said Julian Wyatt, finally resorting to his drink. 'Any ideas where I might look?'

'The country's full of people who want to lend money. Their advertisements are everywhere.'

'The trouble is that they all want some sort of collateral, and all I have is the house which now doesn't belong to us. Can you explain a few financial realities to her, Vernon?'

'Julian is broke,' said Jones. 'I think that's an accurate précis of the situation.'

'I know he's broke,' said Lavinia Wyatt impatiently. 'But that's not going to get me thrown out into the street.'

'For better or for worse, for richer, for poorer,' said Jones.

'A lecture from you on the sanctity of marriage is all I need, Vernon,' said Lavinia Wyatt, giving him a look that quelled for ever a sexual attraction that Jones was just beginning to resurrect. 'How *is* Gaynor?'

'She's gone to the West Country and taken up religion.'

'Poor bitch,' said Lavinia Wyatt. 'She must be desperate.'

Julian Wyatt refilled his glass and dropped money in the till. With two customers, and only one of them drinking, he didn't seem to be providing much help for the Dunbars. A dejected silence hung in the bar.

Eventually, deciding that she was getting nowhere, Lavinia Wyatt stood up and moved towards the door.

'Wayne will be coming to see you,' she said.

Early the following morning after a restless night in which his attempts to sleep ran into the disquieting memory of his manifold problems, Julian Wyatt borrowed the Dunbars' Passat and drove west to see his son.

Speeding down the M3 he wasn't entirely sure why he was making the journey, but now that work had been removed from his life he had had more time to think about Gavin and felt the need to talk to him. Most of the other traffic was holiday-bound, with bikes or boats on the roof, or caravans swaying precariously behind. The sun shone on Stonehenge.

The reminder that this summer there was no holiday
for him did nothing to improve Julian Wyatt's spirits
and he reached Somerset's open spaces wondering what
on earth he was going to tell the boy. He didn't know
how solid the cocky self-confidence of a twelve-year-old
was, but he suspected that it would dissolve like snow
when confronted by something as disturbing as the
parents' divorce.

But to his father's surprise and relief, Gavin, when
he had been extricated from his school for lunch in
Glastonbury, reacted stoically to the disasters that
Julian Wyatt recounted and seemed less hurt than his
father at the way the world was treating them.

'I never thought you were suited,' he declared over
fish and chips. 'This is no surprise to me, Dad.'

'Not suited?' Julian Wyatt said, feeling mildly
stunned. 'Why do you say that?'

'Mummy had boyfriends,' said Gavin.

'You knew?' The indiscretions of his wife seemed
much worse if she hadn't bothered to conceal them
from her son.

'I've got eyes and ears,' said Gavin. 'Anyway, it's no
big deal. Lots of mothers have boyfriends. One's got
eight. And lots of parents get divorced. The mothers
come one weekend, and the fathers the next.'

'And you can handle this, can you? You don't seem
very upset.'

'I've expected it for a long time,' the boy said
impassively. To his father he seemed more like thirty
than twelve, and he began to wonder guiltily what

the influences were that moulded today's children. It was something that he should have concerned himself with before.

'As a matter of fact,' said Gavin, 'I'm surprised that you stayed together so long. Can we have ice cream?'

Julian Wyatt called a waiter, ordered ice cream and drank his tea thoughtfully.

'It's going to make a difference to you, Gavin. For a start, you'll be living in a different house. Ours will have to be sold. It's one of the casualties of the firm collapsing, I'm afraid.'

'And you and Mum will get separate houses?'

'I expect so,' said Julian Wyatt, who couldn't see how he would ever afford a house again.

'I'll be able to choose who I stay with?'

'Of course.'

'It sounds good to me, Dad. It'll only be for a few years because I'm going to Australia remember.'

'You're still set on that, are you?'

'You bet. I've seen it on the soaps.'

Julian Wyatt still couldn't tell whether this phlegmatic display was real or just a front. Had they reared a blond-haired monster who was impervious to grief? Or was he bravely concealing the wretchedness he was feeling? Whichever it was, the school's claim to produce 'confidence without arrogance' seemed to be triumphantly vindicated.

As they drove back to school, Gavin asked him where he was living now.

'I'm staying at the Oasis of Sanity and helping out

the Dunbars. In fact, I've got to get back there to open the bar for them.'

'Do me a favour, Dad,' said Gavin, showing the first hint of alarm. 'Don't let anyone at school know that you're working as a barman.'

19

The man in the grey tracksuit and trainers who jogged along a country lane, watched by docile Friesian cows, a pricket and two foxes, was no longer concerned about whether his health or his blood pressure permitted this level of physical activity or what harm it could do him. He ran along familiar tracks, recognising cowpats and empty drink cans, and waited for signals from his legs, lungs or heart that this gruelling exercise had ceased to be a beneficial way of filling his off-duty hours. But his legs were accustomed to this journey now and covered without protest the green fields and the sandy tracks, jumping fences, climbing stiles and avoiding the pitfalls in crumbling and disregarded lanes.

Julian Wyatt no longer cared whether his body was capable of this strenuous activity or not. He had run this way when he felt worse and, in fact, felt better than when Gerry had taken his blood pressure at the gym. The fresh air and peace of the

empty countryside provided a welcome escape from the
unpleasant appointments that now pressed in on him.
The firm's bank wanted to see him about the house and
his wife's refusal to vacate it, a notice of bankruptcy
proceedings was in the post, the VAT people seemed
to have discovered an unpaid instalment, there was a
writ from an optimistic creditor, his personal bank
had withdrawn his chequebook and credit cards, and
Wayne was coming to see him this evening, according
to an icy phone call he had received that morning from
his wife, for the purpose of inflicting physical damage
of a permanent nature.

It was hard for him to see, as he ran past hedges
turned yellow by primrose and tutsan, how his life
could have collapsed so dramatically and at such speed,
but he knew, as the sweat broke out on his forehead,
that he no longer had the will to reconstruct it. When
he felt a slight constriction in his chest he accelerated
instead of slowing down, defying the fates to do worse
than they had already done.

The disintegration, sudden and all-embracing, had
reached and destroyed every corner of his existence,
from the alarums in his office to the excursions in his
bedroom, and he was still miserably hazy about how
it had happened. A few months ago he was running
a promising and expanding company, he had a family
he imagined to be happy, he had a lovely house and
an expensive vehicle parked proudly in its spacious
garage, and he enjoyed a social life which, while not
extravagant, happily satisfied his leisure hours and

made his efforts worthwhile. Now, without putting a foot wrong, he had lost everything. And, having lost everything, he was about to be punished for it. He went over it all in his mind, trying to identify the moment or move that had produced such fatal and cataclysmic consequences.

A chest pain disturbed his thoughts but he ignored it. His mind roamed through endless conversations with stolid gentlemen in banks. The debts were agreed, the security was provided, the outlook was good. Time would erase the debts and restore the financial stability that both he and the banks were striving for. Or so it had seemed.

The pain stabbed him again and this time it stayed, rising inside him like hot liquid in a cup. He caught his breath, still determined to ignore it and keep running, but breathing was suddenly difficult and the pain was too intense for him to ignore. His body raced on but his legs no longer ran and he left the sandy track and pitched forward into some bushes.

Dear Sir, wrote Emily Mansfield, sitting at a white plastic table on the patio at Rose Cottage. This was a letter that she had wanted to write for some time and she had made unusual preparations for it. Normally her little correctives were scribbled without rehearsal and posted within the hour, but this time she had made notes, changed words and polished phrases. As she sat at the table, she was surrounded by sheets of paper on which she had jotted down portions of this letter when the ideas came to her, and now she had to assemble her stray notes and bring them together in one provocative bulletin. She sipped the cup of tea that she had brought out to help her with this task, and reflected that her handwriting did not get any better. She read what she had written so far. *Dear Sir.* It was an unequivocal start.

As Father's Day approaches and obedient families prepare to dance attendance on their fragile egos, let us pause and contemplate the mystery of men, she wrote.

Deeply flawed, they have an opinion of themselves that is somewhat higher than a non-man can recognise as being even adjacent to the truth. Indeed, truth is often alien to their nature. Occasionally they tell it, as a stopped clock does twice a day, but usually they dissemble unnecessarily in pursuit of an imagined peace in a way that women never do.

Proud of their physical prowess, they are actually feeble and inept. They fall ill, go mad and die first, and even in their prime fall short of the boyish standards they aspire to — if a man's bladder was powered by a muscle as strong as the uterus, he'd be able to pee across the Thames. They lack the silent stoicism of women; when they're in pain everybody has to know about it.

But one of the greatest mysteries about them is their lemming-like talent for self-destruction. Awesome brains collapse at the prospect of sex or tax-free lucre. Lured by money or distracted by a skirt, they have the attention-span of a goldfish with Alzheimer's, and for a moment of pleasure can destroy their careers without a second thought. Surely to God the men who rule the world should be more than itinerant sperm donors?

So far as money is concerned, the more they get, the more they greedily want at whatever personal cost, which accounts for the disproportionate number of millionaires in prison. And when bored they invent daft money-making schemes that bring trouble to themselves and to others.

Can these unfortunate creatures, some of whom I have met personally, be turned into proper people? There are few grounds for hope, but if a caterpillar can turn into a butterfly, anything can happen.

Happy Father's Day!

Emily Mansfield put down her pen and finished her tea. In half an hour she had to collect her husband from the hospital. She would post this letter on her way. It wasn't the sort of thing that he would enjoy reading.

Oscar Mansfield looked like a man who had paid his debt to society and was about to be released from the grimmest dungeon. Balancing on one crutch, he waved the other as his wife approached.

'Get me out of here,' he said. 'I'm innocent.'

'You can't be innocent,' said Emily Mansfield. 'You're a man. Have you mastered those things?'

'If pushed, I can do the mazurka.'

'As long as you can do the washing-up.'

A doctor approached with a clipboard.

'Beware of men carrying clipboards,' said Oscar Mansfield. 'It's a lifelong motto of mine.'

'Hasn't he done well?' said the doctor, a young man who hardly seemed old enough to have left medical school. 'For a man of his age.'

'I'm forty-one,' said Oscar Mansfield sourly. 'It was a broken leg, not senile decay.'

It was a long time since he had spent so much time away from home and he was anxious to get back there. Exposure to complete strangers for twenty-four hours a day had reinforced his conviction that there were a lot of odd people about who should be avoided if he was going to retain any faith in the human race. He had endured their barmy soliloquies and their painfully rambling anecdotes with a patience that only his incapacity could have produced, but all the time he seethed at the asinine conversations that enveloped him. And these were people who were detained here not because of brain damage or a blow to the head, but to repair the straight breakage of a limb. Speculating about the conversations in other wards made him shudder.

'Jones owes me,' he said, when he had lowered himself with difficulty into the front seat of the B.M.W. and taken the crutches that his wife handed him. 'I've had to go through a lot of vexation.'

'I expect you displayed your usual forbearance and tolerance?' his wife suggested as she drove out of the hospital car park.

'No, I didn't,' said Oscar Mansfield. 'I left them in no doubt that I was sharing the ward with idiots.'

'I thought they all seemed to cheer up a bit when you were leaving,' said Emily Mansfield. 'What does Jones owe you?'

'Beer.'

'Beer? And how will you get to the bar?'

'I rather thought that you might drive me.'

'I'll have to see how you behave,' his wife said, patting him on the uninjured leg.

The house was spotless, and hopping from room to room Oscar Mansfield was chastened by the thought that he had not been missed. He went out into the garden, fearing that the product of his diligent labours would have degenerated by now into some sort of nature reserve, but the lawn looked better than when he had last cut it, and the borders had been weeded and hoed.

'You owe Adrian as well,' said Emily Mansfield, coming out to study his progress on crutches. 'He put in a big effort for your return.'

'He's done marvellously,' said Oscar Mansfield. 'How is he?'

'He misses you, I think.'

Oscar Mansfield was touched by this idea which had not occurred to him: the boy had never given any sign that he cared whether Oscar was there or not.

'Well, it's lovely to be home,' he said, kissing his wife. 'Even if you haven't missed me.'

'I've missed you,' she said. 'Particularly at dinner-time and in bed.'

Oscar Mansfield, feeling wanted after all, looked at his watch and hopped to the phone. Jones would be home from college by now, unless he had already gone out. But he answered immediately with some trepidation and then brightened when he heard Oscar's voice.

'I thought it might be my mother-in-law,' he explained. 'Phoning me is her new hobby. Are you home?'

'Home, and ready for the drinks you're going to buy me.'

'I'd be delighted,' said Jones. 'They're letting Colin out this evening, so we can have a little party.'

Oscar Mansfield had completely forgotten that Colin Dunbar had been temporarily stranded in the same hospital. 'How is he?'

'The process of healing is slow,' said Jones solemnly, 'but apparently it can be carried out at home as well as in hospital.'

'I think,' said Oscar Mansfield, 'that this could be a night for champagne.'

In his new forward-looking mood, Jones had nurtured a positive idea: Gaynor, with her newly-discovered religious faith, would now exhibit a saintly indifference to earthly goods, like money, renouncing her half-share in the bungalow's current value with such fervid disdain that he wouldn't actually have to sell it.

But this hope proved to be as evanescent as many others that had misled him over the years, and he was dismayed to find that the mysterious figures with whom she shared these new beliefs had a surpassing interest in banknotes that quite eclipsed the mercenary tendencies of the atheists they condemned. In a matter of days they had collectively hired not one but three lawyers to investigate Jones's assets and divest him of at least half of them. The news filtered back via his mother-in-law that the money was needed to help build a meditation centre, and to print pamphlets and posters of an uplifting nature.

The solicitors demanded a valuation on the bunga-low, or the estate agent's details if it was already on the market. They also wanted the name and address of Jones's own solicitor.

'What sort of church is it, for God's sake?' he demanded during one of his mother-in-law's intermi-nable phone calls.

'I'm not sure it is for God's sake,' she told him. 'It's an esoteric cult with a mystical hierarchy. You know, organic vegetable garden and holistic medicine.'

'No, I don't know,' said Jones. 'It sounds like one of those movements that end up with thirty or forty charred corpses with bullet-holes in the head.'

'I think Gaynor's too sensible to get involved with anything like that.'

'The signs are not good,' said Jones, and went out to find himself a solicitor.

'She walked out on me, I didn't desert her,' he told

the young, bespectacled girl who was assigned to his case. 'Doesn't that affect my financial liabilities?'

'No,' said the girl. 'She's entitled to half the family assets whichever way it went. What's the bungalow worth?'

'In this market? Who knows? It must be down to eighty thousand by now.'

'Get it valued,' said the girl. 'What else is there?'

'There was a car, but she took it.'

'We must remember that. We can knock your half of the value off the final total.'

Jones was uneasy at being given a girl to represent his interests, fearing that she might be in sympathy with the wrong partner in this dispute.

'Her lawyers are talking about adultery. Can't I retaliate and sue for desertion?' he asked hopefully.

'Adultery is quicker,' said the girl.

'It certainly was in my case,' said Jones.

By the time that he got to the Oasis of Sanity that evening, he had provided a guided tour of the bungalow for a valuer from the estate agent who surmised despondently that they would be lucky to get seventy in today's shell-shocked market and urged him, against his own interests, to hang on to the place until things improved.

Oscar Mansfield was sitting on his stool with his crutches propped against the counter. On the next stool was his wife. The promised champagne stood in an ice bucket on the bar. It was not Emily Mansfield's custom to come to the Oasis of Sanity for the simple purpose of consuming liquids; it took the promise of food to produce a personal appearance. Seeing Jones's surprise, she explained: 'I'm here to keep an eye on him.'

'She's also my chauffeuse,' said Oscar Mansfield. 'She's a lady of many talents. So is the ravishing brunette. She'll give you champagne, if you ask her nicely.'

'They're bringing Colin home this evening,' said Fay Dunbar, filling a glass for Jones. She was wearing a dress of brightest red, and was prepared for a reunion. 'Don't make rude remarks about his face.'

'I always do,' said Jones. 'Why should I stop now?'

'It looks a bit like a relief map, but we're told it'll get better. Has anybody seen Julian today? He went out this morning and didn't come back.'

'Banged up with accountants, I should imagine,' said Jones. 'Cheers! Lovely to have you back, Oscar.'

'There were times when I thought I would never make it,' said Oscar Mansfield, with the heavy melodramatic air of a man who has endured much. 'Next time I fall ill, dear, and need internment in hospital, shoot me like a dog.'

'I don't shoot dogs, Oscar,' said Emily Mansfield. 'It's a practice I'm opposed to. Anyway, by the time that Colin gets here it'll be a bit like a hospital ward in this bar. Drink some of Oscar's champagne, Fay. This isn't a Men Only evening.'

'Thanks. I think I will,' said Fay Dunbar, pouring herself a glass. 'I'm worried about what Hannah is going to make of her daddy's face. I'm afraid she'll be frightened.'

'She'll laugh,' said Emily Mansfield. 'Kids are cruel.'

The door opened and Wayne the builder strutted in, wearing the same vest and jeans. He came up to the counter and looked round to check on who was here.

'Is Julian Wyatt about?' he asked, looking at nobody in particular.

Fay Dunbar shook her head. 'He went out this morning and hasn't come back. Do you want a drink while you wait?'

Now Wayne, after a disparaging glance at the available company, shook his head. 'Tell him I called when he appears. He knows why. I'll be back.'

'Who was *that*?' Fay Dunbar asked when he had gone.

'That, would you believe it, is Lavinia Wyatt's fancy man,' said Jones. 'I don't think he came here to do Julian any good. Lavinia is arguing about selling the house, and that man is protecting her interests.'

'If I was Julian, I'd emigrate,' said Oscar Mansfield. 'His life is in a very bad way.'

Jones thought he felt Emily Mansfield's reproachful gaze alight on him when her husband said this and he did not look up. It was inevitable that some people would trace Julian Wyatt's undoing back to the moment when Lavinia tripped seductively into his bungalow — the downfall began there — but Jones did not feel that the blame was entirely his. He was quite prepared to share it with Lavinia Wyatt or even with Julian himself for his injudicious choice of wife.

He lit a cigarette and said: 'I think Julian's life is looking up. He's lost a job that was killing him with worry and overwork, and a wife who was obviously a continuing nightmare. The unpleasant aspects of his existence have been removed. He can only go up from here.'

'Without a bank account?' said Emily Mansfield. 'It'll be a difficult ascent.'

'Well, obviously he should never have married Lavinia,' Jones said. 'Errors like that cost money.'

'When you expose yourself to love, you expose yourself to the risk of pain,' said Emily Mansfield briskly, refilling her glass with Krug champagne. 'It was a risk that became reality in my first marriage.'

'But not in your second,' said Oscar Mansfield.

'The only pain in my second marriage was before we actually got married,' said Emily. 'Oscar used to service my car. It was the most expensive service since the space shuttle *Endeavour* attended to the Hubble telescope in orbit over the earth. I had to marry him to get my money back.'

A car pulled up outside before the bills issued by Oscar Mansfield's garage could receive the scrutiny that his wife felt they deserved, and Colin Dunbar walked in with a male nurse who was carrying his case.

'Colin!' cried Fay Dunbar. 'Wonderful!'

His smile was distorted by the gauze that was still

attached to his cheek, one eye was red and swollen, an eyebrow was missing, his shirt was open to reveal white cloth wrapped round his chest, and the odour of soothing liniment clung to him like cheap aftershave.

'Is it a party?' he asked.

'Colin,' said Oscar Mansfield. 'You've escaped.'

Confronted by medical obstacles, Fay Dunbar abandoned her attempts to kiss her husband and led him instead to a chair on the customers' side of the counter. The nurse left and Colin Dunbar sat down gently. He accepted the champagne that Jones offered him.

'You're talking to a retired chef,' he announced. He sat awkwardly, accommodating the bandages that covered his chest, but his burns, which were superficial by some standards, were not his only wound. Colin Dunbar had developed a pyschological aversion to the Oasis of Sanity and like men who drive miles out of their way to avoid the scene of past follies and disasters, he was anxious to see the back of it. He was vain enough to be worried about his face, and cautious enough to be apprehensive about further duties in the kitchen, but most of all he associated the place with misfortune and failure and he wanted to be rid of it. It was developing into a financial millstone before the fire and it would take a less superstitious man than Colin Dunbar to persist with it now. He had lain for hours in his hospital bed, considering options, selecting and rejecting possible careers, and deliberating over agreeable areas where he could resettle his family. These endless ruminations, disturbed by discomfort

THE MYSTERY OF MEN

and interrupted by pain, had produced not a single idea that he could discuss with his wife, but he held firmly to his original one, that the Oasis of Sanity would only regain its appeal for him when it had a For Sale sign displayed outside.

'Where's Julian?' he asked. 'I thought he was helping you to run this place.'

'He was,' said his wife. 'He's been very good but unfortunately today he seems to have disappeared.'

'He's probably hiding from the gentleman in the vest,' said Oscar Mansfield. 'Lavinia has set her muscular toy boy on him.'

'My God,' said Colin Dunbar. 'What a shambles we all are.'

And sitting at the counter in a huddle they looked like survivors of a natural disaster that had destroyed their homes but left them bruised and alive. Oscar Mansfield, with his crutches, wincing occasionally when he moved his leg, and Colin Dunbar, bravely concealing the pain of his skin graft and the soreness of his face, were the central victims. Jones, whose misfortunes were not in view, appeared untouched by the savage vicissitudes that had afflicted the others, but his expression suggested as usual that he was facing problems of his own.

'I think,' said Fay Dunbar, 'that we'd better have a bottle of champagne on the house.'

'Is it always like this in here?' asked Emily Mansfield. 'I've had more laughs watching *Songs of Praise*.'

'What we have here,' said her husband, 'is an

289

injured and depleted team. You can't expect laughs when we look like the remnants of a casualty ward.'

But the fresh bottle of champagne gradually lifted the spirits of those in the bar and soon Oscar Mansfield and Colin Dunbar were swapping their hospital experiences with the cheerful good humour of army veterans. Jones, excluded from these exchanges, sought to regale the company with an account of his wife's abrupt plunge into outlandish religious beliefs, working in jokes about sex and sects, creed and greed, dogma and doghouse, until even Emily Mansfield smiled.

The good humour was interrupted with dramatic effect. Four youths came in wearing lurid T-shirts which bore the names of various rock bands. They ordered vodkas and rums. Fay Dunbar produced the drinks, took their money and handed them the change.

'Something happened up the road,' said the youth who took the money. 'They found a body in a hedge.'

'Found a body?' said Jones. 'What do you mean?'

'I don't know,' said the youth vaguely. 'There was an ambulance up there near that track that runs along the bottom of the field.'

'Man or woman?' Colin Dunbar asked.

'I don't know,' the youth repeated, and turned with his drinks to the table where his friends were now sitting.

They all looked at each other with the same thought in their heads.

'That's Julian's jogging route,' said Jones. 'I'm going up there.' He put his champagne on the counter and climbed off his stool.

'Jesus,' said Oscar Mansfield. 'What next?'

Confined to the bar by their respective mishaps, he and Colin Dunbar could only sit and wait to see what Jones discovered.

'It would explain his absence,' said Fay. 'He's been so reliable until today.'

A couple came in to share a bottle of wine and retreated with it to a corner, piqued at the less than fulsome welcome they received. The bottle of champagne in the ice bucket on the counter was ignored, as the party atmosphere that had proved so difficult to promote began prematurely to fade.

'My God,' said Emily Mansfield, 'he could have been there since this morning.'

'Hang on, dear,' her husband remonstrated. 'We don't know that it's Julian yet.'

A thoughtful silence fell on them as they kept one eye on the door.

'You're right,' said Emily Mansfield. 'In this day and age it's going to be a woman, just another victim of the growing army of madmen.'

Colin Dunbar and Oscar Mansfield wrestled with the impossible moral quagmire in which they found themselves when they hoped that she was right, but then Oscar's thoughts moved on.

'Another possibility exists,' he said, regretting that drinking seemed by silent consent to have been removed from the evening's programme. 'Lavinia's builder got him.'

A shudder of horror swept over them now as they contemplated the grotesque possibility that Julian Wyatt had been murdered.

'That would make Lavinia an accessory before the fact, kid,' said Colin Dunbar. 'I think this conversation is reaching the realms of fantasy.'

'There are stranger things in the papers every day,' said Emily Mansfield.

'And she's not just talking about her letters to the editor,' said her husband. 'Fill this glass up, Fay. I can't stand the suspense.'

The silence into which they all now fell was broken by the ringing of the phone. Fay, having topped up the glasses, disappeared to answer it, and the silence deepened and broadened as they all sat there waiting helplessly for news.

After three minutes Fay Dunbar, pale and tense, returned to the bar.

'That was Gerry from the gym,' she said quietly. 'They found Julian's body in some bushes half an hour ago.'

'Good God,' said Oscar Mansfield. 'That's it then.'

'He rang in case we didn't know, as Julian was living here.'

'What did he say?' asked Colin Dunbar.

'He said Julian had his tracksuit on and had obviously been jogging. Apparently Gerry had told him not to because of his blood pressure. The theory is that he died this morning, but as he fell in some bushes, no one saw him till this evening.'

An appalled silence gripped the room and even Oscar Mansfield put his drink down.

'Oh God,' said Fay Dunbar, and started to cry.

The door was opened with more force than was normally used to gain entry, and Jones came in with a rush.

'It *was* Julian,' he announced soberly.

'Yes, Vernon,' said Emily Mansfield. 'We know.'

20

The last person into the church a week later, weeping copiously and supported at either elbow by an elderly couple who were taken to be her parents, was Lavinia Wyatt. The three of them progressed slowly up the length of the aisle before she slumped noisily into the pews at the front of the church.

In a row near the back Oscar Mansfield and Emily, Colin Dunbar and Fay, and Vernon Jones sat stiffly in an environment that was alien to them, marvelling at how the vibrant hostility of yesterday could be transformed so easily into today's orgy of grief. Of Gavin Wyatt there was no sign.

The silence was broken by the voice of the vicar, speaking unexpectedly from the back of the church: 'I am the way, the truth and the life: no man cometh unto the Father, but by me.' The procession he led down the aisle towards the altar brought into view the coffin that was covered by flowers.

People who had not been in church for some time, if

at all, listened in sadness and mystification to the recital of a psalm, and a reading from the Bible. Remorse, guilt, relief and disbelief were all silently present.

The vicar, a man in his sixties with sparse grey hair and hollow cheeks who had presided over too many of these sad events to bring any freshness or originality to this one, said a few words.

'I have been told a little bit about Julian,' he began. 'The greatest tribute to him is the number of people who have come here to pay their respects to him today. Jesus said "In my Father's house are many mansions. I go to prepare a place for you". Julian has gone ahead on that road but it is not goodbye. It is only goodbye for a while. In the fullness of time we will all go that way and one day we will meet Julian again.'

'What crap,' hissed Emily Mansfield, seething at the improbability of it in her pew. 'This man's several cents short of a dollar.'

Oscar Mansfield placed a restraining hand on her arm, and was relieved when the congregation burst into a rendition of *Abide With Me*, a hymn that many of them had learned at sporting occasions. It was a hymn that Jones evidently liked, for he alone of their little group contributed vigorously to the singing:

'*Where is death's sting? Where, grave, thy victory?
I triumph still, if Thou abide with me.*'

After prayers, the coffin was lifted up and carried back down the aisle to the graveyard outside. The congregation filed out after it, led by Lavinia Wyatt who held a handkerchief to her eyes, and by the time that the people in the rear pews had reached the graveyard, the vicar was throwing earth into an open grave and grimly intoning: 'Earth to earth, ashes to ashes, dust to dust; in sure and certain hope of the Resurrection to eternal life.'

'All round, not a barrel of laughs,' said Jones, lighting a cigarette. 'I suppose some of these people are Julian's relatives?'

'I don't know who they all are,' said Oscar Mansfield, balancing awkwardly on his crutches. 'He knew a lot of people. Where's his son?'

'Apparently he's fallen out with his mother and wouldn't come with her,' said Fay Dunbar. 'He blames her for everything.'

But they could see, among dozens of wreaths that were strewn round the grave, one that said DADDY in yellow flowers six inches high. The discovery of this brought tears to Fay Dunbar's eyes, and Emily Mansfield was obliged to ask her husband for a handkerchief.

'The funny thing is,' said Oscar Mansfield, 'that it was because of his jogging that I came up with the insurance idea. I wanted a little bet on who would live longer.'

The sensitive subject of the £33,000 they were all about to receive had been discreetly ignored since the discovery of Julian Wyatt's body, and this oblique reference to it now was greeted with embarrassment.

'In America, according to the *New England Journal of Medicine*, forty thousand Americans a year drop dead while exercising,' said Colin Dunbar, pursuing a more acceptable track. His face was now red in patches, but the gauze had been removed.

'That's the sort of statistic Oscar loves, but what he refuses to see is that ten times as many dropped dead when they *weren't* exercising,' said Emily Mansfield.

The five of them moved among the crowd, reading the messages on the wreaths. Poker-faced men and weeping women were making the same painful journey. The open grave had released a flood of emotion that events in the church had failed to stir.

Suddenly, from out of the crowd, they were faced by Lavinia Wyatt, a figure in black but with a white tear-stained face; she looked from her glowering expression as if she would resort to violence if this was not one of the few occasions when nobody could contemplate it. She barred their way with difficulty as her expensive heels sunk into the turf, and directed her remarks at all of them although she was looking at Oscar Mansfield as she spoke.

'I hope you bastards are happy?' she asked with a voice that was close to breaking. 'I hope you all got what you wanted?'

'What are you getting at, Lavinia?' asked Oscar Mansfield, genuinely confused by this unexpected assault.

'You know very well what I'm getting at. The money you have made out of my husband's death. It's obscene. You should all be ashamed.'

The rebuke was delivered with such passion that Oscar Mansfield was temporarily lost for an answer, but Jones's power of speech was not affected by the outburst. He stepped forward, pointing at Lavinia Wyatt with his schoolmasterly finger. 'I resent that very much. There's no rejoicing here, I can tell you. What's obscene is your slanderous implication that we're pleased.'

'You planned it, you lured him into your little scheme. He had to pay a hundred pounds a month that he could no longer afford.' Lavinia Wyatt shook with a ferocity that took them all by surprise, and the possibility that she would soon start hitting somebody still seemed real to them all. 'And now you all clean up! How much is it? Thirty-three thousand each?'

'It's what Julian would have got if any one of us had died,' Oscar Mansfield said, feeling a need to defend himself. 'He was glad to be part of the scheme.'

Fay Dunbar made an unexpected intervention here, primed with information that the others did not possess.

'Lavinia, you're getting a quarter of a million from Julian's insurance, he told me one night in the bar. It was a high-value ten-year policy that paid nothing if he reached fifty.'

'I'm his wife, for God's sake,' said Lavinia Wyatt, with such force that nobody wanted to answer her. 'I have his son to bring up.'

Emily Mansfield, brooding over Gavin's absence, saw her chance to join this unseemly exchange. 'And it's your son that you should be devoting your attention to, Lavinia. Where is he? Not at his father's funeral? He needs you.'

This contribution to the altercation changed the expression on Lavinia Wyatt's face. Distressed by the absence of her son, and disconcerted that it had been noticed, she turned to go. But then she paused, wanting the last word.

'At least,' she said, glaring at Emily Mansfield, 'he doesn't go round peering through people's windows.'

'What a very unpleasant business,' said Jones when she had gone, looking shaken.

'Cast a pall over the whole proceedings,' said Oscar Mansfield. 'We'd better go and have a glass in Julian's memory.'

The man who lies on a sunbed on an island in the Mediterranean six weeks later finds himself in a world he has never expected to see. When he opens his eyes he is looking at a cloudless sky of deepest blue, and when he lazily raises himself to his elbows he can't help noticing that he is surrounded by topless girls, punctilious waiters, tables covered with delicious food and people devoting themselves so assiduously to the business of relaxation that it is hard to imagine that they will ever again adjust to a forty-hour week. He glances admiringly at the brownness of his chest and then resumes his inspection of a girl who is even browner.

Unhindered by considerations that have cramped his

holidays in the past, Jones is here for a month, installed in a luxurious room in the best hotel he could find. He can see now how in the past he has recklessly wasted the long summer holidays from college, often finding himself wishing, with three or four weeks still to go, that he was back at work. This is not going to happen again: holidays will be used as they were intended to be used, for travel, recreation and fun.

He beckons a waiter and orders a *cuba libre* and then picks up the newspaper that lies beneath his sunbed. It is a Sunday newspaper but this is not Sunday. Turning the pages in search of something to read, his eye is caught as usual by the word 'sex', a shaming proclivity which has over the years steered him haplessly towards many wearisome articles on Middlesex, Essex, Sussex, sextons and even sexagenarians.

To men, he reads, *a liaison with the opposite sex is a sort of extra-curricular activity that has no place in the mainstream of their lives*. He lowers the paper, trying to remember where he has heard this sentence before, but it won't come and he lifts the paper again and sees that the article has been written by *Rosie Friedland*. Memories of the cornfield flood back, followed by an almost fatherly relief that the girl is finding success in London. Soon, if she can construct a writing career on one sentence, she will be pontificating in the serious papers on the cultural mores and political cynicism of her unpredictable generation, reviewing films and correcting the Prime Minister's crasser gaffes. He can imagine the articles now. It is all a very great tribute to the man who taught her, who, he realises sipping his drink, is him.

He lies back in the sun, feeling that tiny portion of satisfaction that occasionally comes to people in his job, and then he gets up and dives in the pool. Here he is surrounded by the topless girls he was admiring from his sunbed, but in the water he discovers to his chagrin that although he speaks several languages, theirs is not one of them. Nor does it appear from their boisterous games in the water which exclude him, that Jones is quite what they are looking for.

But nothing can stifle his high spirits now; the travails of the past are behind him. His solicitor, proving a doughtier fighter than he had hoped when he first saw her frail figure behind a desk, has dredged up arguments from obscure books about wives who desert the marital home, and the diminished financial bonanza they can expect. She also anticipates with relish the prospect of producing in court, evidence that Gaynor Jones is now controlled by an occult religious sect which, if the past is any guide, would not only try to take Jones's money, but Gaynor's as well. This idea, that she is protecting the female as well as the male, has given her a motivation that Jones had not expected to find.

He climbs refreshed from the pool and returns to his drink. Tonight, with the security of his £33,000 now earning interest in the bank, he will have dinner in the most expensive restaurant he can find.

One thousand miles to the east, on a cruise liner in the Aegean Sea, Colin Dunbar is having a serious conversation with his daughter. It is an activity that he has had too little time for in the past, and he is determined to give it all his attention. This proves to be a fortunate decision because the eight-year-old's conversational technique seems to be to overwhelm him with questions which tax his powers of imagination and invention, neither of which has been helped by a lunchtime appointment with cloudberry vodka.

'Do fairies talk to animals?' Hannah asks, as if this is a subject that has been troubling her for some time.

'They certainly do,' says Colin Dunbar, picturing the scene. 'Fairies are friendly creatures.'

'What animals do they talk to?'

Colin Dunbar searches his brain. He had not expected the ball to be returned so quickly.

'Rabbits and squirrels mostly,' he declares with the authority of an expert in these matters.

'Not dogs?'

'No,' he says firmly. 'They keep away from dogs.'

'Why? Dogs are nice.'

'Dogs are too big,' he suggests, 'if you're a fairy.'

The ship on which they are travelling is the *Oriana*, which is taking them on an eighteen-day cruise, with stops in Ibiza, Israel, Cyprus, Greece and Turkey. In Israel they have walked along the Via Dolorosa at Jerusalem, in Cyprus they have visited the Troodos Mountains, and soon, in Rhodes, they will stroll through groves of lemons and olives. The trip is costing Colin Dunbar about £6,000, but a cheque for £33,333 which was delivered to him two weeks earlier means that he can face this expense with some nonchalance.

Fay Dunbar emerges from one of the ship's three pools in a white two-piece costume, looking a lot happier than she had ever appeared in the Oasis of Sanity. It is ten days since she has had to cook a meal, ten days, judging by her brown face, spent mostly in the sun.

'I could take a lot of this,' she says, lowering herself on to a sunbed next to her husband. 'It beats two weeks in Brighton.'

'Leisure seems to suit you,' he says. 'It was a mistake to make you work.'

'I'm glad you see it that way. It's not a mistake you are going to make again?'

'Never,' says Colin Dunbar. 'I'll go out and find myself a proper job like other men do. But don't let's talk about that now. It doesn't seem right.'

The sale of the Oasis of Sanity is proceeding smoothly, and only the helpful efforts of the solicitors who are handling it can hold things up. A buyer, or rather two buyers, men of indeterminate gender, appeared from the recessionary fog almost immediately with an offer that exceeded Colin Dunbar's expectations. Tired of city life, they were anxious to find a place together in the country. The business is now referred to by Fay Dunbar as the Oasis of Sodomy.

She gets up and puts a sarong over her swimming

costume. The *Oriana* has a health spa with jacuzzis and saunas, a four-deck atrium with a waterfall, a theatre, a library, a conservatory, a casino, a cinema, a dance floor and countless shops. The largest of her three pools is the biggest afloat.

There is much to do.

In Rose Cottage, tranquillity reigns. There is no desire here to visit distant lands, chat to complete strangers or risk skin cancer by prolonged exposure to the sun. Oscar Mansfield has to prepare his garden for the changing conditions of autumn, and Emily is busy too. Encouraged by columns of reaction to her letter about men, she has other questions and complaints to throw at the world.

Dear Sir, she writes. *You complain that our children do not speak English very well and it is true. But what hope do they have when one of their primary sources of instruction and enlightenment is the television set, whose children's programmes are fronted by youngsters who seem to take a pride in not having mastered the language? I suppose that to select presenters who actually speak English properly would be regarded in these days of pampered minorities as politically incorrect?*

Another matter irks her, and she has no sooner signed one letter than she is into another.

Dear Sir, As our water becomes more expensive, and the price of beer and milk goes ever upward, can anyone tell me why petrol — which is hauled from the ground

*on the other side of the world, processed, refined, and
transported to Britain in gigantic and expensive tankers
and then taken by road to filling stations all over the
country — is the cheapest liquid I can buy? What on
earth do they do to my husband's lager to make it cost
eight times as much?*

These two blasts at a world that is dishonestly run
give her a satisfaction that glows. She puts down her
pen and steps into the garden where her husband is
examining his roses. The crutches have been discarded,
the accident almost forgotten, but when his wife sits
at a table on the patio he is happy to join her.

'What are you going to do, Oscar,' she asks, 'with
your ill-gotten gains?'

'I have no ill-gotten gains,' he protests. 'My
gains have been laboriously, painfully and honestly
acquired.'

'Now that you've got nowhere to drink, I thought
you might build yourself a bar in the garden.'

Oscar Mansfield glances at his wife, a woman who
brims with ideas. A bar in the garden has a certain
novelty appeal, but who would he drink with? He
can see a solitary old man getting drunk on his own
in a shed.

'Is this the thirty-three grand you're talking about?'
he asks.

'The thirty-three thousand that you don't really
need.'

'Ah well,' he says. 'You're right — I don't need it.
So I've given most of it away.'

'You've done *what*?' says Emily Mansfield, feeling a spasm of alarm. 'To whom, may I ask?'

'I began to see the flaw in my scheme. I didn't feel quite right making the money that way, even if Lavinia did collect a quarter of a million from the same unhappy event.'

'I always said it wouldn't bring you much joy. Money has a different feeling, depending on where it came from. Money earned doesn't feel the same as money stolen, and money that has been won doesn't feel like either of them. What have you done with it?'

'I've put twenty thousand in a savings account at the bank in the name of Gavin Wyatt.'

Emily Mansfield leans across and kisses her husband's cheek.

'I always knew it,' she says. 'You're a lovely man, Oscar Mansfield.'

'I always knew it, too. But listen — I've had a new idea.'

Emily Mansfield's loving expression changes with a speed that surprises him. In fact, her look freezes him to his seat.

'Hang on to it, Oscar,' she says. 'Don't tell a soul.'